D1541435

HITLER'S
DESERTERS

HITLER'S DESERTERS
WHEN LAW MERGED WITH TERROR

LARS G. PETERSSON

FONTHILL

Learn more about Fonthill Media. Join our mailing list to find out about our latest titles and special offers at: www.fonthillmedia.com

Fonthill Media Limited
Fonthill Media LLC
www.fonthillmedia.com
office@fonthillmedia.com

First published in the United Kingdom 2013

British Library Cataloguing in Publication Data:
A catalogue record for this book is available from the British Library

ISBN 978-1-78155-269-8

Typeset in 10pt on 13pt Minion Pro
Printed and bound in England
 twitter.com/fonthillmedia facebook.com/fonthillmedia
 #HitlersDeserters

CONTENTS

Acknowledgements

This book would not have been possible without the kind help and support I have so generously been given by three key figures: Ludwig Baumann, Helmut Kober and Peter Schilling. Helmut and Peter are no longer with us, but their memory will stay with me for ever. That these events were not left to be forgotten is thanks mainly to Fritz Wüllner and Manfred Messerschmidt, but I am indebted also to everyone else who has continued to look into this dark part of German history. I am also deeply grateful to Günter Knebel and Ros Kane for their invaluable help in the writing process, and, last but not least, to my wife Josephine for her unfaltering and untiring support.

Lars G. Petersson

About the Author

Lars G. Petersson (b. 1951) is a Swedish-born activist with special interests in peace, mental health, the environment, social justice and animal/human rights. He is the author of a large number of articles and six previous books. Trained as a nurse – specialising in mental health, social issues, and alcohol and substance abuse – he has persistently used his insider knowledge to disclose matters otherwise hidden from public scrutiny. He acquired a thorough understanding of the military as a conscript (trained as a lowest possible grade fighter-plane mechanic) in the Swedish air force at the time of the Cold War and through work in a psychiatric unit under the Danish Department of Defence. For several years he was the co-ordinator of the Danish section of Amnesty International's worldwide anti-death penalty campaign. As a prison nurse, he disclosed severe ill-treatment in custody of (non-criminal) deserters/refugees from both sides of the 1980-88 Iran–Iraq war. This led in 1991 to Denmark being listed for the first time in Amnesty International's annual report on countries with poor human rights records. Lars has gathered extensive knowledge of German politics ever since the early 1970s when he worked as a massage therapist in the state of Hesse. He lives in London with his Irish wife Josephine – his staunchest ally, friend and collaborator. (www.larsgpetersson. com)

Chapter 1

Traitors to the Fatherland

'You fucking pig, traitor to our Fatherland, you fucking coward! Who do you think you are?' He had survived the death sentence and the penal battalion in Ukraine, but now he was met with taunts, jeers and death threats. He had listened to his conscience, and now they called him a pathetic coward. He had refused to comply, therefore they despised him. This was the ultimate punishment for having deserted from the armed forces, those same armed forces that had willingly supported Hitler in attacking his neighbours and had left Europe and huge parts of the rest of the world in smoking ashes and ruins. This was the punishment for running away from the war machinery that had willingly helped a despotic regime to murder millions of innocent people in what, with a chilling shudder, we now call the Holocaust. It was the punishment for going his own way, for using his innate ability to think freely, listen to his conscience and adhere strictly to it.

However, it could have been worse. Hitler's machinery of 'justice' had known no compassion and had condemned the young man to be executed for this 'terrible crime'. Only a number of coincidences and good personal connections had saved this twenty-one-year-old German's life from being terminated in front of a firing squad, beneath the axe or on the gallows.

Over half a century has passed since then. The bombed-out ruins have been rebuilt and the Marshall Plan implemented; even the Cold War is now over and the reunification of East and West Germany has long been completed. These events all belong to history. But Ludwig Baumann, a man entering the autumn of his life, is still for many a despised coward, who let down not only his comrades but also his country. Moreover, according to German law, Baumann – the last known surviving Hitler deserter – together with all his now dead co-victims of the Nazi war judges, until recently was legally an ex-convict, a man with a criminal past.

The refugee

The sun had passed its highest point and the shadows were getting longer. In fact, Peter Schilling, another fugitive from Nazi Germany at war, could not have covered that long a distance since setting out early in the morning. He recalled: 'It was more and more difficult to get started again after each break. But I just had to keep going. There was no other way, and I kept telling myself it couldn't be that far to the border. Maybe behind the next hill?' He was walking from tree to tree, around open fields and meadows, taking care not to give himself away, but he had already been on the run for six hours or more. In fact, it was only a guess; it wasn't that important. It was more about staying safe. He had to listen for signs of danger and look for movements or anything suspicious in his surroundings, for strategic positions where guards could be placed. 'Sure, they are not only to be found in the immediate vicinity of the border but also here in the hinterland', he thought to himself. Guards and patrols on the move could have been anywhere.

And, as he was also aware, he was not the only human being forced to flee across the border. The border patrols were definitely not waiting only for him. In fact, they probably knew nothing about him, this young traitor and deserter who was trying to run away. After all, as he put it himself many years later:

> There were so many they were looking for; there were so many on the wanted list: criminals of all kinds, thieves, murderers, deserters, saboteurs and spies, not forgetting Communists. Maybe, on this particular day, they had put out an extraordinarily fine net, waiting for some big fish? Maybe they were hunting someone very important, maybe a first class enemy of the state? For them, I was only third class, a nobody. There were so many on the run, so many they were trying to stop running away.

It has been estimated that close to 50,000 German soldiers deserted from their units during the Second World War. However, such disloyalty was not accepted, and severe measures had been prepared long before the battles even started. 'For desertion in the field the harshest measures must be taken', was the edict from highest command in both the military and party. 'Desertion is and will remain the worst crime a German soldier can ever commit.' These were the orders and they would be strictly adhered to: 30,000 of these deserters and military offenders would be sentenced to death.

Of these men, around 20,000 were to be executed, the majority by shooting but in some cases by beheading or hanging. The remaining 10,000 – those who, for one reason or another, had had their death sentences commuted to long prison sentences – were transferred to concentration camps or more often to special military units called penal battalions, as the prison sentence in these cases was postponed to be served after the war had ended. However, this was in no way to be seen as leniency; transfer to a penal battalion was practically equivalent to a (new) death sentence, as the chance of surviving there was close to non-existent. Many a man was killed in these units' 'express journey to heaven commandos'. As the nickname implies, the men were sent on extremely dangerous and frequently pointless military operations. The worse the war prospects became for the German side and the more threatening the inevitable catastrophe looked for Hitler's army, the more energetic the war tribunals became and the more 'offenders' were sent to the Eastern Front as cannon-fodder for these units.

However, disobedience was a problem not only for the army; it was the same for the air force and the navy. The navy judges were even stricter than the others, and, not least when Germany was close to final defeat, they showed no compassion. To understand why the admiralty in particular feared any attempted mutiny, we need to look back to

A deserter faces the firing squad.

the history of the First World War. It is very likely that the reason for the extreme cruelty the judges showed when they dealt with disobedient seamen at the end of the Second World War can be found in some of the admirals' experiences from the final days of the Great War.

In 1918, when the war was nearly over and it was obvious that continued fighting was pointless and would only lead to further meaningless death and destruction, something happened in Wilhelmshaven that, for a country still at war, was unusual: the sailors went on strike. They refused to leave the port for more battles. Most simply left their battleships and joined the factory workers on the streets. Together they forced an end to the slaughter. That was the final humiliation for Wilhelm II. He had no choice but to abdicate. After the tyrannical Kaiser's subsequent escape to Holland, the war ended and Germany became a republic. Hitler and Admiral Raeder were in full agreement: something like that should never be allowed to happen again. Therefore, any attempted mutiny would be nipped in the bud. No mercy would be shown.

Soldiers, airmen and sailors were sentenced to death mainly for deserting, but there could be countless other reasons that led to execution. If there was any doubt about which paragraph to use against an internal enemy, one could always justify any allegation with what Nazi war justice called *Wehrkraftzersetzung* – 'undermining or drastically reducing the German people's spirit to defend the country'. The number of possible offences that could be covered by this exceptionally elastic legal paragraph was without limits. Soldiers charged under this legislation could be accused of having slandered the Führer, weakened the armed forces, shown lack of courage on the battlefield, given assistance in one way or another to the enemy, self-inflicted wounds, listened to forbidden radio transmitters, commented negatively about the war (even in a private conversation) or 'procured access to alien possessions'.

The last crime mentioned here covered such offences as the theft of a pair of socks to keep the cold at bay during the cold winter months of the Russian campaign. A young soldier named Julius had disobeyed the Führer's orders regarding winter outfits and accessories for the Eastern Front. On a cold January night in 1942, he had taken eight pairs of woollen socks and one neck scarf for himself and his comrades. His penalty was death by shooting. *Wehrkraftzersetzung* was a terror law meant to terrorise, and it did its job.

Apart from those unfortunate thousands of defectors mentioned above, there were others who escaped and were not caught. It is estimated that during the war there were close to 10,000 German soldiers who succeeded in their attempts to defect to the enemy. They were never prosecuted and punished. The official number of deserters therefore includes only those who were sentenced for their actions and not all those thousands who successfully defected to the enemy or went into hiding. In addition, it does not include all those who disappeared from their units in the final months of the war, when hundreds of thousands of soldiers left as the German army broke down and dissolved. Many of these people were hanged on the spot, without any questions asked, if they were unlucky enough to be apprehended by the military police. Hanging from trees or lamp posts with a 'COWARD' sign around the neck, they functioned as a warning to others not to leave the sinking ship. Technically all these men were also deserters, but because the war was almost over, they never appeared in the statistics and annals of the Nazi war tribunals, and so this story is not primarily about them.

At the end of the war there were 1.3 million sentenced soldiers who were subsequently regarded as ex-convicts. They had all been prosecuted and sentenced by the over 1,000 war tribunals which had been in action all over the country as well as in the occupied territories and aboard warships. About 4,000 of those who had originally been given the harshest penalty possible but for some reason had had their sentence commuted also survived their stays in concentration camps and penal battalions.

Though most of these men would have been destroyed in body and soul, they would still have had reason to hope for a better future and for justice. At least they would have expected a more or less immediate rehabilitation of their honour, maybe even an official acknowledgement of what they had done. This was, however, not to be. After the war they would continue to be seen as cowards and traitors to their Fatherland; they would be subjected to jibes, smears and outright threats. For most of these men there was no other way than to try to hide their past, to escape once again. They would continue to pay a high price, and for most this meant for the rest of their lives. Only a handful ever lived long enough to see a half-hearted rehabilitation law passed by the *Bundestag*, more than half a century later.

Chapter 2

Shot at Dawn

Adolf Hitler and his henchmen had had a very good reason to guard the borders very carefully and prevent escapes like Peter Schilling's. They had also had good reason to prepare themselves carefully against any internal resistance within the armed forces. The dictator had been aware of this risk to his war plans ever since he himself served as a corporal in the First World War. Inspired by what had taken place there on both sides of the trenches, he had made up his mind about what to do with potential deserters and conscientious objectors – ideas which would later have lethal consequences for his victims to come.

'Those who are not with us are against us,' Hitler famously claimed, but he had been much more specific than that. In his prison cell after the failed coup attempt in 1923, he wrote in what would later become the infamous *Mein Kampf*:

> If one intends to keep cowardly men to their duties, then there is only one option. The deserter must know that his desertion will have exactly the same consequence as that which he is trying to escape. At the front you can die; as a deserter you shall die. Draconian measures such as the death penalty are the only means to deter would-be deserters.

The former corporal had learned his lesson and had come to his conclusion: a merciless war justice would secure his success and lead Germany to victory in the coming war. His perception of what had led to the Fatherland's painful defeat in 1918 was clear and now he proclaimed: 'Only one state has never made use of the articles of its existing war law and this state disintegrated. This state was Germany. This laxness shall not be repeated!' From 1914 to 1918, German war tribunals had sentenced 'only' 150 men to death, and out of them 'only' forty-eight (seventeen deserters) had been executed. In those facts he found the reason for the humiliating defeat. Hitler's idea was that the German war courts during the 'Great' War had been much too lenient and forgiving. This, according to the future dictator, was the reason why German soldiers had lost their morale, and in the end lost the war. The opposite, he claimed, had been the case on the enemy side, and that had finally made them successful.

Whether or not the sheer number of troops killed by their own comrades on orders from above actually had decided the First World War is questionable, to put it mildly, but Hitler was right when he compared war court statistics: the numbers of sentenced and executed British soldiers were both roughly ten times higher than those of their German counterparts; if all the Triple Entente forces were included in the calculation, the difference between the two sides of the war would be massive. But I do not have those numbers, so will leave it there, as the figures we already have speak for themselves.

During the First World War, 3,080 British and Commonwealth troops were sentenced to death by war judges. 'Only' some ten per cent of them, 346, were finally executed, but that is still ten times the German figure for the same war, enough to inspire Hitler and, in his mind, justify his theories. Here it is important to stress that we are talking about a war fought mainly by the underclass on behalf of the upper class's imagined needs for territorial expansion and power, unlike the war that was to follow, which primarily would be an act of genocide based on an extremely evil ideology, supported and made possible by the *Wehrmacht* institution and its military conquests. Still, and this is my point, when getting down to details about how 'cowards' were treated, it is not difficult to find similarities. As this book, more than anything else, is about ordinary people being exploited as pawns in the elite's belligerent game playing, we must never forget that no side has a complete monopoly on malignity.

Owing to the specific character of the First World War, a large number of men were mentally numbed by the immense stress of being in permanent danger of imminent death or mutilation. The intolerable fear and the gruesome conditions, the squalor, the sight of so much death, the expectation to endure the unendurable, all this drove men to the edge of madness and beyond. Mental health got a new diagnosis: shell shock. As in most wars (and Hitler would learn it here), it was about keeping up morale among one's own troops – in plain English, to scare any thought of resistance out of them before it ever popped up. And for that purpose, as usual, examples were needed of what would happen to those who would not toe the line.

I do not know whether the future German dictator ever knew of the following case; I think not, but if he had, it could have been used as a perfect teaching example for his future system of terror justice. On the Somme on 26 November 1916, British troops in thick mist came under heavy mortar fire. Sergeant W. Stones went out on a patrol with a lieutenant and suddenly came face to face with the enemy. The lieutenant was shot dead and Stones ran back to raise the alarm. In the panic he had lost his rifle and, though he had escaped the pursuing Germans and made it back to his own lines unhurt, this would in the end cost him his life. When it was discovered that he had returned unarmed, he was arrested for 'shamefully throwing away his weapon', court-martialled, sentenced to death and executed by his own comrades in arms.

This was nothing unusual but more or less standard procedure: men who only days before might have fought at his side in the trenches would now be ordered to line up and take his life in cold blood. That was all according to the protocol, as was the rest of the routine. After Field Marshal Sir Douglas Haig had confirmed a death sentence, in this case Sergeant Stones', the man would be informed and at dawn the following morning he would be tied to a pole and shot dead by a firing squad consisting of around six fellow soldiers. However, before that final action could take its course, medicine and the church would play their parts as well. First a medical officer would pin a piece of white cloth over the man's heart, as if that job would require the qualifications of a doctor and as if it in the most remote way could have been in accord with the Hippocratic Oath, and then a priest would read a prayer – in order to complete a circus that can only be described as an act of premeditated murder.

As examples of what kind of 'men' we will also find when looking into the list of young British and Commonwealth soldiers who exited the world in this manner, it might be interesting to note the names of two privates, A. Evans and J. Byers. They were both no more than sixteen when they were tried by judges and subsequently executed. These *children*, and many others with them (we will come back to that), were among the 306 British and Commonwealth soldiers who were executed after having been found guilty by British courts martial of offences such as cowardice, desertion and throwing away arms. On top of that, another forty soldiers were sentenced and executed for treason and other unspecified crimes – whatever they could have been.

The most well-known case of a British soldier shot at dawn during the First Word War is that of Pte Harry Farr. Farr was twenty-five when he was executed in October 1916. Before the final incident that led to his death, he had spent two full years at the front and was badly affected by his experiences. Twice he had been admitted to hospital in France for shell shock, the last time shortly before his final breakdown. Being classed as 'fit' again, Farr was ordered, during the Battle of the Somme, to take rations to the front line. On his way, hearing and seeing exploding shells falling on the trenches, he suddenly panicked and refused to continue – an act of disobedience that would lead to his death. In his trial, at the Field General Court Martial at Ville-sur-Ancre on 2 October 1916, this soldier did not even have a defence lawyer; the badly traumatised man had to defend himself. Even this was not unusual; many soldiers were not legally represented during these trials, though most of them were suffering severely from shell shock and/or post-traumatic stress disorder.

Harry Farr, from 1st Battalion West Yorkshire Regiment, was charged under Section 4(7) of the Army Act 1881 for 'misbehaving before the enemy in such a manner as to show cowardice'. In a court presided over by Lt Col. F. Spring and including two other members, a captain and a lieutenant, it was obvious that he, a young man of limited education and without a defence lawyer, in a trial that was, as most others, to last no more than twenty minutes, stood no chance against officers from a different part of society. Four days later, Lt Gen. Cavan, the 10th Earl of Cavan, pronounced the final verdict on Pte Farr: death by firing squad, no pardon. 'I certify that the sentence was duly carried out at Carnoy at 6 a.m. on 18 October 1916. (signed) A. J. D. Simey Captain A.P.M. VI Divn.' These were the final words in a document confirming that Harry Farr was no more.

Other documents from the process have been duly accessed from the archives, and much of them show the mind-set of the people involved in his predetermined death. In the trial documents I was astonished to find statements such as: 'I cannot say what has destroyed this man's nerves, but he has proved himself on many occasions incapable of keeping his head in action & likely [sic] to cause a panic.' This was a statement by one of the prosecutor's witnesses – indeed, an extraordinary comment under these

Harry Farr.

circumstances. The words of Lt Gen. Cavan, whose final decision sealed Pte Farr's fate, speak for themselves: 'The charge of cowardice seems to be clearly proved & the Sergt. Major's opinion of the man is definitely bad to say the least of it. The G.O.C. 6th Div. informs me that the men know the man is no good. I therefore recommend that the sentence be carried out.'

Apart from the way they were killed, these men had one particular thing in common: they were almost exclusively from the lower ranks; only two were officers. This was the ordinary man's offence – very much because it was the ordinary men, not the high officers, who would face the grenades and explosions. And, just as would be the case on the German side in the war that was to follow, it would be the ordinary man's widow and fatherless children who would be left without compensation for the loss of their breadwinner. The letter from the War Office in London to Pte Farr's young widow was short:

Dear Madam,

We regret to inform you that your husband has died. He was sentenced for cowardice and was shot at dawn on 18 October.

That was all it said, nothing more. Following that, the young widow was thrown out of her accommodation with her little child.

Harry was twenty-five when he died. More than a hundred of his executed soldier-friends had been below the age of nineteen; four of them were no more than sixteen. They were nothing but children. If they were not children themselves, when killed by their own state for nothing more serious than being afraid, they might have been fathers to some who were. And, if so, then the punishment would not stop with the firing squad: the bereaved children and their mothers would also continue to be punished by being excluded in very hard times from possible means of financial support – the war pension they would otherwise have been entitled to had the man been killed in the 'right way'.

Harry Farr had first enlisted two years before the war, and had served another two years in France under the most difficult circumstances. But all that was now seen as worthless because in the end his nerves could no longer cope with the unrelenting slaughter and carnage. His widow, Gertrude, was left alone to fend for her child. As we can see, it was not thanks to the War Office's 'care' for the families left behind but despite it that she managed a very difficult situation. Thanks to good luck she found work with a very friendly lord and his kind family. They accepted the new maid and her little daughter almost as part of the family and by this means Gertrude got through the immediate hard post-war years. Later, she married again. However, the tragedy would in a way repeat itself: Hitler's war would make her a widow for the second time. Her new husband, whose lungs had been severely damaged by poison gas in the First World War, was killed in the second conflict.

It took many years for Harry Farr's story to be told to his only child. Gertie grew up believing her dad had been killed in action, as nothing else was said other than he had died in France. She got to know what had actually happened only when in her early forties: 'My mother had been too ashamed to tell me, but knowing now what had happened explained a lot of things that had made her very sad over the years.'

The secret, however, continued well into the next generation. It remained under wraps in the family and it was only when Janet, Harry's granddaughter, started to research the family tree that the wound opened up fully. She wanted to visit her grandfather's grave in France, but when her mother was asked for information about where to find it, she had to admit that she did not know; she had to admit that the father she had never known, as he had left for France when she was only a small baby, had no known grave. She had no idea where he had been put to rest, and Janet would now be told why.

This was the start of Janet Booth's fifteen-year-long campaign to have her grandfather – and, by extension, all 306 victims – pardoned by the British Government. Harry Farr's widow never lived to see it, but thanks to his granddaughter, his daughter did. Of course, a memorial and a posthumous pardon cannot change much for those whose lives were taken away from them in such a brutal way. But for those left behind, especially for a little girl grown into an old woman, with her upcoming centenary more or less coinciding with that of the war that killed her grandfather, it meant the closure of a painful old wound.

'I am proud of being his daughter,' Gertie, now Mrs Gertie Harris, said as she unveiled the Shot at Dawn memorial during a ceremony in June 2001 at the National Memorial Arboretum in Alrewas, Staffordshire. No less proud was her own daughter Janet, the granddaughter who had spent years of her life fighting for the pardon of her grandfather. 'Remember, Lars,' she said when I was about to leave, after having spent a sunny spring afternoon at her home in Surrey, talking about what had happened all these years ago, 'my grandfather was no coward; he even refused to be blindfolded.'

Harry Farr might have been defenceless at the court martial and he was defenceless in front of the firing squad, but he had met them all with open eyes and 'he had been a fine soldier'. The family knew that and had found comfort in that statement. The priest who had been present at the execution had made the effort to ask the local vicar in London to go and tell the bereaved wife. These words had for years been a consolation not only for Harry Farr's widow but later also for his daughter and granddaughter. Unfortunately, his death and those of the other 305 commemorated war victims at Alrewas would inspire the biggest judicial mass murder the world has ever seen.

Chapter 3

Back to Work

If German war courts had, according to some, been too lenient during the First World War, it became worse after the November Revolution in 1918. The special system of law with specific articles for soldiers was abolished and a new order was written into the constitution of the nascent Weimar Republic. This for some people was unthinkable. The abolition of military tribunals led to the unemployment of the Emperor's war judges, whose harsh opposition towards the new Republic was therefore evident from the very beginning of the inter-war years. They were keen to return to the previous situation as soon as possible. Many of these military lawyers, being strong early supporters of Hitler, shared his view that, in wartime, harsher methods were required in the meting out of justice.

A remedy to the 'catastrophe' emerged soon after the Nazis came to power. No doubt to the pleasure of these jobless lawyers, a new policy was put forward in 1933. Hitler, in line with his firm beliefs and plans for the future, began to press for the re-establishment of the war tribunal system, and immediately after the new minister, Lt Gen. Werner von Blomberg, had taken up his position, preparations for new laws began. Lawyers set to work rigorously, preparing legislation that was intended to lead to a new age in German military justice. With severe penalties in place, any disobedient soldier would be terrorised into submission.

As early as 24 April 1933, Minister Blomberg presented his proposal to the cabinet and justified it with the following reasoning:

> As the political circumstances throughout Germany have changed, the time has come to resurrect the military system of justice. This we do, not only in order to extinguish the dangers to the military which would be a consequence of war but also to give to the revamped armed forces what is absolutely necessary in terms of the system of justice.

Only three weeks later, on 12 May, the law for the re-establishment of these tribunals was passed in parliament and the earlier war judges could now return to their esteemed careers. The military justice introduced at that time, however, was not to contain any of the fundamental principles of a fair trial as we know it today. There was no right of appeal and no right to a defence lawyer. This legal system had the exclusive purpose of frightening soldiers into submission and thus enabling Hitler to achieve his military goals. It clearly and unequivocally contributed to stabilising Nazi power and prolonged the war that followed.

The so-called lenient military courts during the First World War bore a great responsibility for the German defeat, the Nazis claimed, and constant reminders of this defeat were a vital part of their propaganda. Hitler had no difficulty in finding support among the military judges, who all gladly supported his views and willingly began to live up to his expectations.

In 1934, Reich President Hindenburg's death was followed by a referendum in which an overwhelming majority of the German people approved the proposal to combine the posts of president of the republic and chancellor under one hat, Adolf Hitler's. The turnout of voters was enormous: 95 per cent of the electorate took part, and 90 per cent of them were in favour. As the Nazi administration already had legislative powers according to the recent Enabling Act, this referendum made the former corporal into a dictator – an elected one. It was obvious that the people wanted it that way.

I swear by the Lord this holy oath

The next important step in completing Hitler's unquestioned power would be the introduction of a rewritten oath of loyalty to which all officers, conscripts and other armed forces staff as well as all public servants (in a slightly different version) would be bound. It was not a new oath but an amended version of an existing one. However, the change in the text was remarkable. In two steps the words had been changed to fit the need. During the Weimar Republic the oath of loyalty would have been sworn to the constitution, the *Reichsverfassung*; from 1933 it would have been to the 'people and Fatherland', but with the final change in 1934 it was turned into an oath of loyalty to Adolf Hitler in person:

> *Ich schwöre bei Gott diesen heiligen Eid, daß ich dem Führer des Deutschen Reiches und Volkes, Adolf Hitler, dem Obersten Befehlshaber der Wehrmacht, unbedingten Gehorsam leisten und als tapferer Soldat bereit sein will, jederzeit für diesen Eid mein Leben einzusetzen.*

> (I swear by the Lord this holy oath, that I will show unconditional obedience to Adolf Hitler, Führer of the German Reich and people and commander-in-chief of the armed forces, and that I, as a brave soldier, at any time am ready to sacrifice my life for this oath.)

With this oath, every single individual connected to the armed forces, from generals to privates, was personally bound to Hitler. Thus was built the foundation for what would follow – a path to catastrophe for the German people.

An unworthy life

There is a little hollow in the meadow scenery out there. It could be water but I must move over 50 metres into open land to reach it and that could lead to them spotting me. This bloody thirst is jeopardising it all! Shall I leave this fragile cover just because

I can't control myself any longer? Maybe there's nothing out there either, but I can't think about anything but water. Why can't I just stop thinking of it? No, it is there in my brain. It is embedded there and now I can't do anything but think about getting something to drink. I am going mad due to lack of water.

Oh my God, out there in front of me is water! I don't need to crawl out into that meadow, beside me right there is a little puddle! And the water is clean and cool and tastes fresh. I drink and drink; with both hands I form a bowl, throw the water in my face, over my hair and feel the shivering as it runs down my back. And I drink till my stomach is absolutely full. I could keep drinking till evening. Yes, I could stay here until it's all over when I don't have to fear any longer. A quarter of an hour, half an hour or maybe it's only five minutes and then the inertia is gone.

Hours later, Peter Schilling peers out of the bushes, glancing from side to side. With no time to think, he swiftly jumps through the prickly branches, then scuttles along the road, under the wire fence and into the glen. He squeezes his face down in the dry grass and listens but senses nothing: no commandos, no life-ending bang from a carbine, only his beating heart and a blackbird that sings its evening song for him.

This fence is the border and they can blast you down like a wild dog. This ridiculous wire! Why doesn't that bloody bird stop singing? Take it easy, don't hurry, maybe there's a signal wire in between that will reveal my whereabouts or maybe even mines … Oh, what if the border is mined! My God, the wire has thousands of barbs! Careful, squeeze yourself tightly, like a serpent, crawl alongside the brook and quietly in between the high trees. I embrace a tree. I've managed it! The war is behind me. My God, I am alive, I am alive!

After Peter had realised that the German expansion plan was an appalling crime, he decided to escape. His Second World War story, however, did not end with him safely reaching the Swiss border; we will meet him again. But, luckily enough, fate would be good to this young man: he did survive the war. Many others, not necessarily all heroic resistance fighters, were not so fortunate.

One of them was twenty-four-year-old Anton from regiment 462, who had fought for four years at the Eastern Front without any significant break. 'Encouraging in battle,' his commander had praised him. For his outstanding efforts, he had been made non-commissioned officer and given twenty-one days' special leave. While at home with his wife and child, he met his sister's boyfriend who filled him with wine before telling him, 'Anton, don't be stupid and return to the front!' Half drunk, Anton let himself be injected with kerosene, and the same night he was taken seriously ill as a result of the toxic effects and admitted to the local hospital. It was six weeks before he was sufficiently recovered to be able to face the war tribunal and be sentenced to death for self-mutilation.

Ferdinand was different. He was physically weak and suffered from chronic ill-health. Although only sixteen years old, he had already been a soldier for four weeks when what would seal his fate happened. Fourteen days before the Russians marched into Vienna on 13 April 1945, a war tribunal sentenced the boy to death for desertion. But Ferdinand had not left his post in order to escape – during an enemy bomb attack he had suffered a nervous breakdown. He had only *planned* an escape after spending a number of desperate days under military arrest due to that breakdown.

But Ferdinand's pathetic state was no reason for the judge to show mercy. 'He looks spineless and immature,' the court stated during the presentation of evidence. 'The personal impression of the defendant is that of a childish-looking boy.' At sentencing, this fact – that the defendant actually *was* a boy, a child – changed nothing. Both Ferdinand and Anton were sentenced and had to pay with their lives because their judges adhered to the radical Nazi idea of extreme discipline and deterrence. The mistakes from the First World War must not be repeated. 'A soldier can die, a deserter shall die.'

Young Karl was on his very first war mission with his battalion and for days they had been under heavy fire close to the Polish town of Warka. Even at night he had no rest, and he also experienced constant hunger due to the scarcity of provisions. These battle conditions were so severe that few eighteen-year-old boys would have been mature or experienced enough to handle them. When a close friend in the trench was fatally wounded, Karl lost his head and shot himself in the right hand. The penalty for this self-mutilation was death. Karl had committed a crime during battle, 'in a situation of emergency for the German people, when we depend on every single man.' When the sentence was passed, it was stated that the overriding importance of deterrence made clemency out of the question. 'Why,' asked the judge, 'should society tolerate such an individual at a time when the best of German blood is flowing in the war?'

This concept of deterrence was not to be found anywhere in the legal texts, but the lawyers, eager to help Hitler and his war, found a way to implement their own policies with great zeal. Expressions such as 'sub-human' and 'useless life' were widely used to defend and motivate their inhuman sentences. This was completely in line with the thinking of the Nazi ideologists who, supported by lawyers and psychiatrists, produced a picture of worthless psychopaths to whom all clemency must be denied. Others, those who suffered from mental health problems, were seen as fully responsible for their own mental state. The psychiatrist Schneider was extremely inventive in his diagnoses, declaring that those who had insufficient desire to recover with the help of therapeutic input were committing *Wehrkraftzersetzung* and should be punished.

According to psychiatric reports, the young soldier Paul undoubtedly belonged to a group of human beings who would today be classified as suffering from moderate learning disability. However, the judge failed to take this fact into account and, despite Paul's very low IQ, maintained that there was no reason why such a person should receive a more lenient sentence. In fact, it was the other way around: poor mental health and/or low intelligence would have been seen in these courts as aggravating rather than mitigating circumstances. 'Why should such useless individuals who are burdens to society get special treatment? What value is he or others like him to the military?'

Sufferers from physical diseases were not necessarily better off. One 'criminal' suffered from asthma, and this condition made his situation, when facing the court, even worse. The prosecutor declared, 'This is no mitigating circumstance, only an aggravating one, and if this person is pardoned he will simply be a burden to society.' This view among military lawyers was exactly in line with the dominant Nazi ideology.

Chapter 4

Right is What the Führer Wants

On a dark night in June 1942, twenty-year-old Ludwig Baumann deserted with his friend, twenty-two-year-old Kurt Oldenburg, from their navy base in the French port of Bordeaux. 'We didn't want to be part of this murdering war; we didn't want to kill people; we wanted to live.' Ludwig does not see himself as a hero. He was young; he wanted to live and was scared of dying. Today he says: 'Why should I go to a foreign country and shoot people who have never wronged me?'

The following day the two friends were arrested by a German patrol at the border of Vichy France, the unoccupied part of France. Despite the fact that they were both armed, they were not willing to use their weapons against others by shooting their way out of their predicament. They let themselves be arrested without resistance. 'We just couldn't kill.'

Ludwig and Kurt, both from Hamburg, had broken up a cache of arms and stolen some weapons and ammunition aboard a ship while preparing the escape. It was night and local French friends were waiting for them nearby with a small lorry ready to drive them to a place near the demarcation line. The plan was that they would flee over the border before dawn:

> The Frenchmen left and we made our way towards the border. However, we ran straight into the arms of a German custom patrol. They found us strange and suspicious, but, as we had changed into civilian clothes in the lorry, berets and all, they took us for unarmed Frenchmen and led us back to their headquarters for interrogation.
>
> It was a remarkable situation. They walked in front of us with their rifles hanging over their shoulders and we had loaded pistols in our pockets. We could have shot them but we didn't. We had armed ourselves in order to feel safe but today I still feel safer unarmed, despite having received several death threats since the war. When we arrived at the customs office it was disastrous. We couldn't speak French and now our path of suffering and anguish began.

This anguish has never ended for Ludwig Baumann. While I write these lines, seventy-one years after this ill-fated rendezvous between the two young deserters and the outstretched arm of Nazi military law, Ludwig is still with us, and what was done to him so many years ago still fills him with terror. He had been totally unprepared for what would happen to him and Kurt that night and in the years to come. It was different with the system he suddenly

Kurt Oldenburg.

was up against. As we know, Hitler had made his plan for how to deal with traitors like these two young men, and the methods had all been meticulously prepared. The system was now ready to deal with its prey. It did not look good for the two young men.

So let us have a look at the law behind it all. The basic legislation regulating this area consisted of two important statutes implemented in 1938: the so-called War Special Penalty Statute of Justice (*Kriegssonderstrafrechtsverordnung*) and the War Penalty Statute (*Kriegsstrafverfahrensordnung*). The first laid down the basis of the war courts, and the second introduced a shortened processing of cases without right of appeal to a higher court. It was all about keeping up morale.

Refusal of military service on grounds of conscience was of course totally unacceptable but was only one of a number of reasons for punishing soldiers with death. In one of the statutes it was highlighted which criminals should be punished in this way. Among other things it was decided that those who self-mutilated or 'in one way or another' withdrew themselves from duty would fall into this category. 'In one way or another', according to the additions to the clause, could mean somebody who had intercourse with a prostitute in the hope of getting a sexually transmitted illness that could hinder his war duty, or one who committed an ordinary crime in order to postpone the draft.

In the general eagerness to come to terms with disloyal citizens, the military lawyers also discussed whether a suicide attempt should be seen as self-mutilation – or even as desertion. If so, it should be punished as such. The general opinion was that this was the case if it could be assumed that the criminal had taken into account that, in case he was saved, he might have made himself unusable for military service.

All courts possessed the power over life and death, and the chance of a successful appeal was strictly limited, though a system was in place. The rule was that all sentences should be confirmed by the *Gerichtherr*, the jurisdiction holder who was also the commander-in-chief of the division. However, this system rarely benefited the sentenced soldier. It was more commonly the other way around: a prison term was found too lenient and was changed into a death sentence by the general or admiral.

We must remember that this was not about justice. The role of the judges was merely to serve the system, not to seek the truth. The fear of punishment should be so great among soldiers that any act that breached the rules should be prevented because of fear of the consequences. There was consensus among the judges that this could be achieved only by the threat, and frequent use, of the death penalty. In order to achieve this, the legal experts had worked secretly and intensively to sharpen a number of special rules and introduce new ones.

> Members of the Jehovah's Witnesses and related groups who refused to serve as soldiers before the war were generally sentenced to one or two years in prison or concentration camp. At the start of the war, a more serious punishment was introduced. From then on, any objector, as well as any person who instigated somebody else to refuse war service, was to be punished with death. On 15 September 1939, August Dickmann became the first member of the Jehovah's Witnesses to be executed for refusing to serve in the *Wehrmacht*. He was followed by many others. The estimate is that around 270 members of this church had their lives cut short by Hitler's judges for the same reason. Today these men would be considered as conscientious objectors, but in post-war Germany they were not recognised as victims of the Nazi regime.

Until the outbreak of the Second World War, this process led to extreme elasticity in the new laws. Apart from *Wehrkraftzersetzung* (undermining the morale of the people), these laws were *Treuebruch* (breach of faith) and *Verrat an der kämpfenden Volksgemeinschaft* (treason against the struggling people), just to mention a few. *Wehrkraftzersetzung* was probably the worst of them all. It was a crime that covered almost anything. It could be any disturbance or attempt to influence in a negative way the state of alert of the nation. Its basis was more or less 'Right is what the Führer wants'.

In connection with this legal development, the *Reichkriegsgerich*, the Supreme Military Court, was established in 1936 as the highest level of justice within the armed forces. Later, during the war, it was to move from its original site in Berlin-Charlottenburg to the Zieten barracks in the fortressed town of Torgau by the Elbe, about 50 kilometres north-east of Leipzig. A photograph taken a few years later in this little town in Saxony would become world famous. It shows Soviet and American soldiers who, on 25 April 1945, met on the bridge across the river shortly before they triumphed over the last remnants of the Third Reich and liberated Germany and the world from Nazi supremacy.

This picture, more than any other, symbolises the end of the Second World War, but unfortunately it was only one of many pictures of Torgau. The town, with its 30,000 inhabitants, also has another history, far more sinister than a famous handshake on a bridge. Apart from the already mentioned Supreme Military Court it would also be home to two of the eight Nazi military prisons in Germany. They were located in the local prison Fort Zinna and fortress Brückenkopf respectively. As the infamous penalty

US lieutenant Bill Robertson and Soviet sergeant Nikolaj Andrejev shake hands on the bombed Elbe bridge at Torgau, 25 April 1945.

camps *Feldstraflager 1 and 2* – often referred to as military concentration camps – could also be found here, camps in which prisoners were often killed arbitrarily and died from hunger and ill treatment, it is easy to see that Torgau willingly or unwillingly became the capital of Nazi war justice. In fact, the town became synonymous with the hunting down and persecution of deserters and other offenders from the German armed forces. As was the case for so many other young men, Torgau also came to play a huge and destructive role in the life of Ludwig Baumann.

Chapter 5

Hell in Fort Zinna

It was right after the reintroduction of conscription on 21 May 1935 that Fort Zinna, which until then had served as an ordinary penitentiary, was changed into a military prison, the biggest in Nazi Germany. Thereafter this grim place was to be much worse than it had ever been before; it became a centre of constant hunger, harassment and torture, a hell-hole where severe maltreatment followed the slightest infringement of internal despotic rules. All kinds of shocking abuse took place here, including murder. Absolute contempt for human dignity was an everyday occurrence behind these walls.

Generally there were only two ways out of this institution – dead, after having been executed or having died from some other reason, or, if 'lucky', transfer to a penal battalion, a so-called probation unit, *Bewährungseinheit*. Having ended up in such a military unit, a soldier who had had a death sentence commuted to life in prison would be on 'probation', i.e. he would get another chance, as it was said, to prove himself worthy at the front to live in the Fatherland in spite of the awful crime he had committed against the state. By demonstrating exemplary behaviour and courage he would be given the chance to be reintegrated into the community. However, only a few prisoners achieved this 'privilege', as their chances of survival in these units were close to zero. To be moved to a *Bewährungseinheit* was, in reality, the same as a new death sentence.

This was completely in line with the ruling policy, as the Nazis believed that it would be outrageous if a war boycotter could happily and safely serve his sentence at a time when those who had stayed loyal to the cause suffered heroes' deaths on the battlefield. 'Honourless men and cowards should be given no chance to escape front-line duty!' declared the high commanders within the armed forces, and here they had support from Hitler's statute 'Postponement of Penalty for the Benefit of *Bewährung*' (21 December 1940). This statute ordered the postponement of a sentence until after the end of the war so that the culprit could be given a 'chance to redeem himself'. He would be prevented from escaping his duties at the front.

Ludwig Baumann was among those in one of these units who got an opportunity to prove himself worthy of life, though – as these troops were routinely sent on extremely dangerous suicidal missions – the chance that he would also survive that ordeal was minimal. Ludwig recollects:

> We were put in there, where everything on the Eastern Front had broken down. Our troops used the 'scorched earth' policy. Villages were burnt down, civilians were

Fort Zinna in 1938.

massacred and we were thrown in right there to cover the retreat and delay the enemy. We were badly armed and malnourished and defecting to the enemy was more or less impossible. A German soldier could not expect humane treatment from the Russians at a time when they regained their lost territories and found their civilians dead and the earth burned.

Sentenced to death

Ludwig Baumann was born on 13 December 1921. He had a sister, Gertrud, who was three years older. Their parents both came from poor backgrounds but, despite that, their father Otto, a tobacco wholesaler, had built up a successful business and reached a respectable position in Hamburg-Eilbek where the family lived. It was his wish that one day his son would take over the business.

But Ludwig was different. When he started school, difficulties arose because he suffered from dyslexia. 'I had to fight and struggle for hours every day. Childhood was not easy for me, but', as he says now, 'if you were well behaved and toed the line, happiness would follow.' Apart from that, there were difficult times also on the national level. As we know by now, a new party had entered the stage, and many were impressed

Ludwig (second from left in front row) and his sister, Gertrud (standing, fifth from left).

by it – including Ludwig's father. Like so many others, he had voted for Hitler and the Nazis in the last free election of November 1932. This, however, he bitterly regretted shortly after. Ludwig's father was definitely no Nazi, but, as Ludwig recalls, very conservative.

Otto Baumann had been born in 1888, had adored Kaiser Wilhelm, served in the navy in Kiel during the First World War and now, like many others, for a short while, he had followed the view: 'Better Nazism with law and order than Socialism or Communism heading straight for disaster.' However, this view, as he later came to realise, was a direct path to the same disaster he had wanted to avoid; in fact, one much worse than he could ever have imagined.

Yet, before that was to happen, Ludwig was hit by a personal catastrophe that was to affect him deeply and push everything else into the background. Only the year before, he had started an apprenticeship as a bricklayer in the hope of a secure future, when this dream was suddenly ripped apart by a personal tragedy: his mother Thea was killed in a traffic accident. Ludwig was fifteen and, as he realises now so many years later, it was a time when his need for maternal love had been at its greatest. The effect on the young boy was tremendous:

It is true that I have good memories of my father, but there was something very special about my mother. I still miss her so much to this very day. I think my world broke down the day my mother died. I did not understand the intensity of my grief. I started to refuse to do anything I didn't want to do. If I didn't want to do something, I simply didn't do it, and that would include what my father would ask me to do.

Ludwig was not alone: all young people who did not join were subject to intense pressure. If, for example, non-members wished to study, they were put at the end of the queue, though not completely excluded. Sought-after academic disciplines such as medicine and law, however, were completely out of reach. Many people could therefore honestly state that they had joined the Nazi party in order to be able to study. Nonetheless, in 1936 the law was changed and it became obligatory for all children aged fourteen to join either the *Hitler Jugend* or *Bund Deutscher Mädel* (the League of German Girls).

Ludwig Baumann was conscripted to the navy in 1940, aged nineteen. He definitely did not belong to those who headed zealously for the battlefield. His recruitment training had taken place in Belgium, and after that he had been transferred with his unit to the French coastal town of Gravelines between Calais and Dunkirk. The plan was that the Germans – in rebuilt inland vessels with support from the Luftwaffe, the air force – should cross the Channel in good weather and invade England. There were hundreds, maybe thousands, of these inland vessels spread over many small towns and canals.

But, as it turned out, it would not be that easy. While practising for the planned invasion, Ludwig was exposed for the first time to what war would be like. The British knew what was going on and consequently the ships were often attacked by the RAF's Spitfires, leading to many casualties. In the end it was obvious that air supremacy was not on the German side but on the British, so the whole project had no chance of success and was abandoned. Instead Ludwig was transferred to Bordeaux where a new harbour unit was established.

Soon after entering military service, Ludwig became a problem for his sergeants as he refused to polish their boots and carry out other orders. They took brutal revenge with exhausting exercise and extra guard duties:

> They terrorised me so badly, I was absolutely traumatised at that point and the memories have haunted me ever since. I knew what was in store for me when I refused orders but still I refused; I just couldn't comply.

The harbour company to which he had been transferred consisted of those conscripts who could not be used elsewhere; people who, in one way or another, did not live up to expectations. According to Ludwig, they were decent men, but from a military point of view more or less useless. For the time being that did not matter much: they had been assigned to guard the port, but there was not much to guard, as all the ports around were blockaded by the Allies.

> We became good friends with the dockers, firefighters and the French guards at the harbour, and at that time the idea of deserting came into our minds. I don't know if it came from us or from them; I don t remember. Close by there was a demarcation line, a kind of border. At this time a non-occupied part of France existed, and getting there was our first goal. The French resistance fighters had supplied us with names and addresses and the plan was that from this free part of France we would head for the USA via Morocco.

Why did I desert? I think life as a soldier embodies a total lack of freedom accompanied by constant degradation. Hitler's forces, of course, embraced the extreme end of the scale, but it is also partly true of army life today. I also had other reasons. For example, Hitler's repeated media propaganda for *Lebensraum* [more space for the German people] was not justified in my eyes. Even if I was totally apolitical, I still asked myself questions like: 'What is all this about? What about those people who already live there? Are they to be exterminated or driven into exile?' These issues constantly occupied my mind.

The German forces assaulted one European country after another and finally the Soviet Union. They had tremendous success initially and advanced all the way to Moscow. The Soviet army was surrounded, and in the cinema we saw pictures from Kiev where hundreds of thousands of Soviet prisoners of war were huddled into huge open fields. Then the cold Russian winter came and many people, including Germans, froze to death. Extensive collections of clothing were organised in Germany. But these clothes were intended for German soldiers only and at that time many of us sat down and discussed the fate of the prisoners of war. We asked ourselves: 'Will they all freeze and starve to death?' Yes, many, maybe most of them, did. At that time some of us said: 'No, we don't want to be part of this anymore. This is a war crime! We will not be part of this genocide.'

Ludwig Baumann deserted on 3 June 1942, and it was on 30 June that he was sentenced to death after a court hearing lasting only forty minutes. 'We were tortured during interrogation and also later in the death cells, as we continued to refuse to name our French friends who had helped us.' Ludwig was also sentenced for 'watch duty slackness' – as a few months before deserting he had fallen asleep during guard duty, and serious theft – as, while preparing for the escape, he had stolen two pistols, nine packets of ammunition and a torch.

'Baumann did not flee because of an opposing stance to Hitler, but because he tried to avoid being punished,' it was stated in his sentence, and this was part of the basis for the judge's hard stance. 'For desertion the most serious punishment must be used,' he wrote, before concluding:

Desertion is and remains the most disgraceful crime a German soldier can commit. No fear of punishment for committed offences can justify a soldier taking such action. Even if pardon might be considered, such a thought must not hinder a war court from looking for and passing the correct punishment. He who deserts in companionship with others and tries to flee abroad and he who commits crimes during the escape must be punished with death – all according to the guidelines from the highest command of the *Wehrmacht* 14 April 1940 Ziff. I Abs. 2. Only under other circumstances can a prison sentence be considered as proper punishment. [...] The war court therefore must sentence both defendants [Ludwig and Kurt] to death.

Navy war court in western France, department Royan, 'In the name of the German people: in the criminal case against Evalt Gronewold, Kurt Oldenburg and

Gericht des Marinebefehlshabers
Westfrankreich, Zweigstelle
R o y a n .

J. X 271 - 272 - 309/42.

F e l d u r t e i l

im Namen des Deutschen Volkes.

In der Strafsache gegen die Matr. Gefr. Evalt Gronewold
und Matr.Gefr. Kurt Oldenburg und M.A. Gefr. Ludwig
Baumann

vom Kommando Hafen-Komp. Bordeaux

wegen Fahnenflucht im Felde, Wachverfehlung im Felde und
schweren Diebstahls

hat ein am 3o. Juni 1942 in Bordeaux

auf Befehl des Gerichtsherrn und Marinebefehlshabers Westfrankreich

zusammengetretenes Feldkriegsgericht,

an dem teilgenommen haben:

als Richter:

1.) Marinekriegsgerichtsrat Dr. Lüder
                              Verhandlungsleiter,
2.) Kapt.Lt. Harders, (M.A.),
3.) Masch.Gefr. Albrecht

            als Vertreter der Anklage:

Marinekriegsgerichtsrat Mönkemeier

            als Urkundsbeamter der Geschäftsstelle:

Schreibers-Gefr. Jussen

für Recht erkannt:

    Es werden verurteilt

    der Angeklagte Groenewold wegen Wachverfehlung im Felde
    in Tateinheit mit schwerem Diebstahl zu

        1 1/2 - eineinhalb - Jahr Gefängnis.

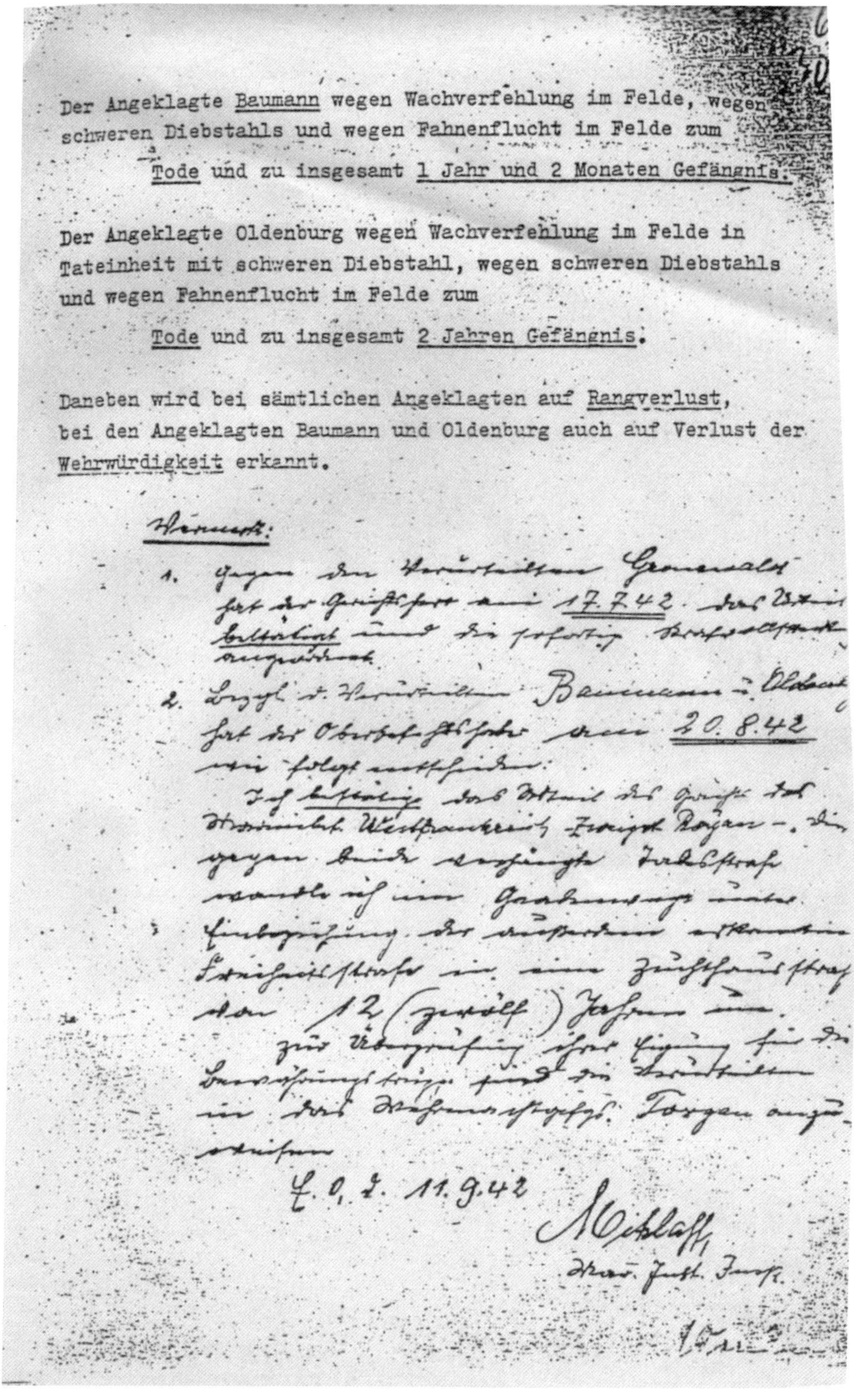

Der Angeklagte Baumann wegen Wachverfehlung im Felde, wegen schweren Diebstahls und wegen Fahnenflucht im Felde zum

Tode und zu insgesamt 1 Jahr und 2 Monaten Gefängnis.

Der Angeklagte Oldenburg wegen Wachverfehlung im Felde in Tateinheit mit schweren Diebstahl, wegen schweren Diebstahls und wegen Fahnenflucht im Felde zum

Tode und zu insgesamt 2 Jahren Gefängnis.

Daneben wird bei sämtlichen Angeklagten auf Rangverlust, bei den Angeklagten Baumann und Oldenburg auch auf Verlust der Wehrwürdigkeit erkannt.

Ludwig's death sentence.

Ludwig Baumann, all from the harbour company in Bordeaux, the court, under the chairmanship of Dr Lüder, has sentenced defendant Gronewold for neglect of guard duty in the field and for serious theft to one and a half years' imprisonment, and defendant Baumann for neglect of guard duty, serious theft and desertion to death and to one year and two months' imprisonment. The defendant Oldenburg is sentenced to death and to two years' imprisonment for neglect of guard duty in connection with serious theft, for serious theft and for desertion.'

Chapter 6

When Law Merged with Terror

A legal front-runner

After his graduation in 1926, the young lawyer Erich Schwinge proceeded to a postgraduate degree in law at the University of Bonn. That same year he accepted a position in Kiel and from 1932 he worked in Halle. In 1936, Schwinge chose military law as his professional speciality and was offered a position in Marburg where he developed into a writer of law texts. Schwinge was a theorist and thrived in his new job; he wrote legal commentaries on the Military Criminal Code (*Militärstrafgesetzbuch*) and his contributions and ideas would have huge importance for the military court system in the coming war. He was highly successful, and some of his work soon became the most widely used publications on the subject.

In particular, one legal commentary that he wrote stands out as extraordinary. It shows with utmost clarity what kind of person Schwinge was. As an instruction for the military judges, he wrote:

> It is expected from a [Nazi war] judge that he will adapt the law to what is the view and what is requested by the state at any given time – also if that means going further [in severity] than the lawmakers had intended.

'It was in 1945, only two weeks before the end of the war. I served in a pioneer unit. We were not far from the town of Neisse [today known as Nysa in Woiwodschaft Oppeln, Poland]. Not far from us were the Riesengebirge [Karkonosze] mountains, which were the destination for many deserters. One soldier in the unit, around twenty-one years of age, was mentally completely finished. We all knew that the war would soon be over, but the boy – for me he was just a big child – deserted, ran away. For sure, he was soon captured and sentenced to death. During my years at the Eastern Front I had seen a lot of dying, but this boy I shall never forget. The whole company was commanded to attend. They dragged him to the pole and tied him to it. The firing squad waited for the order to fire. Facing imminent death, the boy kept screaming for his mother; he cried and begged for his life. In this way our youth died, allegedly for the Führer and the Fatherland.'

Tönnies Hellmann

Erich Schwinge.

In the years that followed, Schwinge's ideas would firmly guide military tribunals in passing sentences. On rare occasions when lawyers were having second thoughts in handing out death sentences to deserters or other offenders in the armed forces, it was always easy to refer back to and seek justification in the publications of this man – and that would not be in favour of leniency. As one of the most authoritative authors of Nazi military law, Schwinge had a tremendous influence on the entire system, and in his world compassion had no place. In his view, harsh penalties were the basis for a powerful and effective army. One of his 'truths' was: 'Only one acquittal at a critical time could have the effect of totally destroying the fighting morale within the troops.'

According to Schwinge, a soldier had 'an enhanced duty to accept danger', and in line with that view he favoured frequent use of the death penalty for people who did not live up to expectations. The deterrent aspect of imminent and certain death was here of supreme importance: 'Only in this way could necessary discipline and full control over the armed forces be enforced.' However, he had thought of another method as well. He supported the transfer to special units at the front of 'psychopaths' and those 'inferior beings who show a lack of strength and power of endurance', as well as of those who had committed crimes like desertion, refusal to follow orders, and malingering. This was essential so that the ordinary troops could be separated from those scum, it was said. Following that, the earlier mentioned penal battalions were established, all in line with Schwinge's theories.

In 1941, Schwinge was also given an ideal opportunity to put his theoretical ideas into practice when he accepted a new position at the University of Vienna. In addition to his work as a lecturer, he was from then on also given the opportunity to act at war courts – not only locally but also in France, Belgium and Ukraine. As prosecutor and judge in these countries, he was personally responsible for sixteen young soldiers' deaths. The sentence in the case against Anton Reschny is the one that has left the most powerful impression.

Two weeks after he was drafted into the military, seventeen-year-old Reschny stole a purse and two watches whilst assisting in the clearing out of houses about to collapse. As a consequence of this minor misdemeanour he ended up in front of Judge Schwinge, accused of exploiting the war situation and of theft. For this crime, the young boy 'only' faced a maximum of ten years' imprisonment. However, Schwinge was inventive; he altered the accusation to 'pilfering in action', used the 'Guidelines for Military Law' (written by himself) and, according to the principles of *Manneszucht* (hard discipline) and *Abschreckung* (deterrence), he could now condemn the young Reschny to death. It is remarkable that this sentence was finally commuted to fifteen years in prison by none other than *Reichsführer-SS* Heinrich Himmler!

Reschny survived the war and forty years later he sued the judge for twisting the law and attempted murder because of the discrepancy between the offence and the outrageous sentence imposed. However, the prosecution in Marburg adjourned the case and an appeal to a higher court was dismissed. The last appeal, to the Supreme Court of the state of Hesse, was also turned down, but the decision was at least accompanied by the comment that the sentence had been 'very harsh'. However, as Schwinge, as the basis for his sentence, had used commentaries from the military books of justice (written, of course, by himself) he had not made himself Lord over life and death. He had been supported by the law texts, it was said in the final statements of the court.

The last death sentence for which Schwinge was responsible was imposed on 9 February 1945, only a few months before the end of the war. The victim was Josef, a thirty-five-year-old corporal who was accused of *Wehrkraftzersetzung* – in this case, evading duty by self-mutilation. Josef had injected himself with kerosene. Even Schwinge recognised several mitigating circumstances but callously decided not to let them have any influence on the final verdict.

The verdict reads:

> At the sentencing the war court has asked itself if this case could be seen as a less serious offence. Surely the untainted reputation of the accused, his good behaviour as a soldier, his expression of remorse, his confession and his demeanour in court, not to mention that he is the last survivor of three sons, should be taken into account. But, the court is still of the opinion that the prevailing situation forbids us from showing any leniency.

Judge Schwinge's written statement, which sealed the fate of this young soldier, ends thus:

> In an extremely critical situation, the defendant has removed himself from the front and thereby shown his comrades a very bad and dangerous example. Such negligence

can, in the interest of discipline, only be punished by the strongest possible measure, which is death.

The road to Torgau

After the news of Ludwig's death sentence had reached his father, Otto Baumann applied for clemency on his son's behalf. He also approached a business friend who happened to be a friend of no less a person than Erich Raeder, the chief in command of the navy. Merchant Robinson and Grand Admiral Raeder had served as officer colleagues during the First World War. After that they had gone different ways professionally: Raeder had continued his military career in the heavily restricted armed forces under the Weimar Republic, and Robinson had chosen business. But the two men had remained friends, enjoying hunting together.

Having considered the case carefully, Raeder reporting back to his friend that he 'in no way could let personal relationships have any influence on his professional decisions' but that he had pardoned both Baumann and Oldenburg. In his letter, Raeder wrote: 'Now it is the duty of Baumann and Oldenburg to show the Führer courage and spirit, thereby showing that they deserved to be pardoned.'

Grand Admiral Erich Raeder.

Grand Admiral Erich Raeder was the commander-in-chief of the German navy between 1935 and 1943. At the Nuremberg Trials, he was sentenced to life in prison but was released in 1955. Raeder's successor was Admiral Karl Dönitz who succeeded the Führer after Hitler had committed suicide.

After becoming commander-in-chief of the navy, Dönitz issued the clear instruction that under him no deserter must ever be pardoned. Unlike the army and the air force, where around thirty per cent of the death sentences were commuted (the condemned men then died in the penal battalions instead), in the navy very few men were given a second chance.

Ludwig's sentence was commuted and he was instead given a twelve-year prison term to be served after the war, assuming a German victory. Until then he and Kurt would spend time in concentration camps or penal battalions. The prisoners themselves, however, were not told. First, after having spent eight months in their death cells, with both hands and feet in shackles, they were informed of their new chance to live. Therefore, every morning for a total of ten months they had to live with the fear that the executioners were on their way.

Day and night they lay in their shackles, and every morning as the guards changed, Ludwig waited nervously for his executioner to come. For around 240 days he woke up with the knowledge it could be his last. But, as if that was not enough, it was not the only regular threat that plagued his day in that grim place. He was also physically tortured. It was not only because Ludwig had refused to identify the French people who had helped him and Kurt to leave the naval base; with other detainees, Spanish hostages, he had also been planning an escape.

There were many Spaniards in the prison. They were known as 'red Spaniards' because as Communists they had fled from Franco. First they had found protection in southern France, but that was to turn out to be not much better than what they had escaped from. Soon the Germans occupied the country and the refugees found themselves in the arms of a new tormentor. If a German soldier was shot, the occupying troops arrested local people at random and executed them in retaliation. In this way, these Spaniards had ended up as hostages and prisoners.

There were about ninety such Spaniards in the prison at the time Ludwig was there, many of them children aged no more than ten or eleven – and they were all to be killed. Relatives of the hostages were brought in to the prison yard in order to bid farewell to their loved ones:

Through the bars of my cell window I could see mothers and wives take their men and children in their arms. Thereafter I could hear them scream as they refused to let go. I could see how *Wehrmacht* soldiers brutally pulled them apart. They were all shot, also the children. At that moment I became politicised.

In the death cell I was given permission to receive mail once a month, one letter, and I was also allowed to write one. In the letters to my father it was clear that I did not know of my pardon and this made him anxious. The arrival of mail every time was an extremely anxious event for my father, as he continually feared news of my execution. Every morning as the guards changed I was petrified they would come for me. It was such an unbearably cruel experience that it has constantly haunted me ever since, and I am still traumatised to this very day.

Although his sentence was commuted on 20 August 1942, it was not until 29 April 1943 that he and Kurt were taken to the prison governor of Bordeaux and told of the decision. Only later was he also made aware of the family's efforts leading up to this disclosure. Like Ludwig, his father was also dyslexic, and it had therefore been his sister who, in their father's name, had written to the commander of the German navy in western France:

Referring to your letter to me, which I have attached, I allow myself with utmost respect to write to you regarding the sentencing of my son. As my son does not know about the granting of pardon, I myself have begun to doubt as to whether or not the decision is being upheld or not. I therefore ask you most politely to let me know if the commutation of the sentence by Herr Grand Admiral Raeder to twelve years' penitentiary has been changed or is still in effect. Yours sincerely …

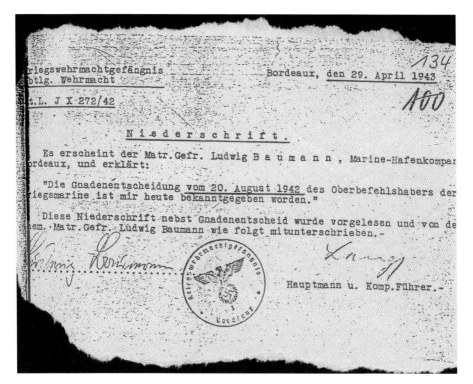

'I have today been notified of the decision to grant me a pardon.' This document was presented to Ludwig Baumann ten months after the decision had been taken, and was subsequently signed by him and the commander of the prison.

Ludwig Baumann was thereafter first transferred to the concentration camp at Esterwegen and then to the military prison of Fort Zinna in Torgau. On arrival, he suffered from diphtheria and was put in quarantine. 'I stayed there for over a year, as I couldn't walk. As a consequence of my ill health, not only was my voice paralysed but also my legs.' Although Ludwig could not speak or walk, his condition did not spare him from experiencing all the misery that was part of Torgau, including the executions. He and his comrades were forced to attend and watch.

The death candidates all wore shackles on their hands and feet, just as Ludwig had in his own death cell. These irons are now exhibited among torture instruments from the Middle Ages in the fortress's museum, reminding us of man's unceasingly inventive gift for cruelty.

As we changed clothing, we were occasionally given jackets with a small hole at the front and a big hole at the back, chilling evidence of our friends' awful fate. Today all these abhorrent memories continue to haunt me in my dreams.

Another witness to a deserter's execution at Fort Zinna recalls:

The poor man got the whole load in his breast and sank down but was still alive, groaning horribly. At last the staff sergeant came up to him and finished him off. That was horrendous for us to witness; he shot him twice in the head.

Chapter 7

If Only the Führer Had Known …

Peter Schilling's father could not understand him, and this lack of understanding was mutual. '"You have a disastrous tendency for taking the wrong road; you lack style, culture and a sense of pride," he bitterly rebuked me,' Peter recalled. Then, shortly afterwards, his father would comment on the status of the family:

'We the Schillings are the best. We have nothing in common with Pletis and Kretis. If you sleep with dogs you rise with fleas. I forbid you to mix with such riff-raff. Furthermore the vicar's children should be role models for the community and should in turn look for their own proper role models.'

Peter continued:

Relentless preaching of morality was very much a feature in the home growing up, and I regularly had my ears boxed to enforce the message. There were constant lectures about chivalry, decency and etiquette.

This home was a German vicarage of the 1920s and '30s. It was here that the young escapee in the wood spent his formative years, and the society of which it was a part was the same as the one in which the ultimate evil of the Nazi movement was to be created. When, years ago, I listened to Peter Schilling's story about his childhood and adolescence, it struck me how much a child's world can mirror that of grown-ups:

That church was the centre of another village. It was a dreadful little place full of uncivilised, thick, dirty, lazy and backward villagers. They were absolute riff-raff, totally different from us. Maybe there were a few exceptions, but they were never mentioned. On the other hand, it was quite good that this revolting village with its uncouth inhabitants existed. If they hadn't been there, how would we have known our own superiority? Bad eggs are always the others, never oneself, friends or loved ones, and such scum made it easy to spot one's own good qualities and character. As these people were not some of ours, they were automatically our enemies, our inherited foes since time immemorial, and on and off there was 'war' between us. We had a legitimate right to attack their filthy village and steal their apples as we saw fit – even if they, of course, were inferior to our own.

Yes, it had almost sounded like a child's preparation for life as a real soldier, attacking not only villages but other countries. And, as we know, so it would end. Instead of war games against the neighbouring riff-raff community, it would be Poland, France and others with them.

For Peter's grandfather it was important for a man to be fit and able, ready to answer a call to such duties whenever it came. Regrettably for him, he never became a soldier himself. A stiff leg as the result of an accident in his youth had thwarted his desire for a military career. In his heart, however, he was a warrior and very proud of his three sons – Fritz, Theo and Jochen – who had been decorated during the First World War for their valiant efforts for Kaiser and Fatherland.

Within the family circle, his grandfather was a respected authority. He was the steady rock to rely on, and nobody questioned his opinions. As Peter remembers: 'Grandfather was Prussian, a devout Christian, God-fearing, upright, pure in mind, yes, straight from a storybook.' But he was also clear that although the old man always had been strictly loyal to the concept of authority, a Nazi supporter or follower he was not. The self-righteousness of these people was repulsive to him. Hence, like so many Germans of his time, he often said: *'Wenn das der Führer wüsste'* ('If only the Führer had known'). He, the Führer, was always part of his grandfather's religious services and was included in his grace before meals; Adolf Hitler was always prayed for in the same vein as distant relatives.

This was all very much in line with the times, or, as Peter Schilling expressed it: 'To challenge figures of authority would for grandfather have been the same as blaspheming the will of the almighty God Himself.' In other words, it would have been impossible, out of the question. Five of this man's grandchildren lost their lives on the battlefields of the Second World War, and his prayer in response was, 'Lord, I thank you for having accepted those martyrs of the Fatherland.' His unshakeable belief in the goodness of God was absolutely steadfast.

Much later, Peter realised that he himself had received a special role in these prayers. When, in the summer of 1943, he had been turned into a traitor to the Fatherland, the Gestapo went looking for him everywhere possible and of course also in his relatives' homes. His grandfather's vicarage was not exempt from that search, and this made him extremely upset. Peter said:

> How could they have the audacity to think that he could ever hide me or know where I was hidden? That's how he was thinking. He was a good German with no understanding of treason. 'Please, Lord,' he prayed, 'please say that it is not true. Please, Lord, tell me that he has been ripped to shreds by an enemy bomb so that he cannot bring such shame upon us. If you punish us with such a dreadful shame, my Lord, please give us a sign as to why we deserved such suffering and show us how to be forgiven.'

To have a traitor to the Fatherland among his own family would for Peter's grandfather have been an unbearable thought; but now it had happened.

In a way, this man must also have been a victim of his time, a victim of a society where the establishment was not to be questioned. As Peter remembered from his youth, it was not possible to discuss Christianity or religion with his grandfather. One should believe in God and the commandments without questioning, period. And when it came to the Fatherland and the God-given rights of the ruling class, there was nothing to question there either. They were chosen by God, and by the mercy of God they carried out his will.

With this wisdom and conviction he shuffled untouched and with great pride through life. I cannot criticise him for that because that was his genuine view. It was not surprising that I, as a deserter, in 1943 was the embodiment of evil, a sinner against the unchangeable laws of God, according to his world view.

Prepare for war

'If you want peace you have to prepare yourself for war.' In the Latin lessons we were brainwashed with this idea from an old Roman saying; we swallowed it without reflecting on the real meaning of the words, and there were no opposing voices to be heard. I was no different from all the others. We were all inspired by the Führer and his closest associates' heroic speeches. At that time it was my intention to make a career as an army officer so that I too could live a heroic life myself and be admired and respected. The glorified virtues of soldiering that our teachers talked about were from me and my friends' point of view absolutely worth living and dying for.

The tension kept increasing and the propaganda did its job, both in the schools, as described above, and in the rest of society. Hardly a day passed without reports in the newspapers and on the radio about the (alleged) murder and maltreatment of ethnic Germans in Poland. When Hitler then finally declared the invasion, there were very few objections. It was as if something inevitable had happened, and it was met with enthusiasm. Schoolchildren were lined up to greet with songs and cheers the passing columns of soldiers, motorbikes, cars, light armour and artillery – and all of society joined in. 'How envious we were!' Peter remembered. 'I will join the army willingly,' his friend Bernhard declared. 'That's what we'll all do!' was the answer. Both boys exclaimed with delight: 'We'll join now, otherwise this war will finish without us.'

Peter recalled, 'Our geography and gymnastics teacher, Herr Seidal, was a violent thug. Boxing pupils on the ears was his method of teaching us the exact geographical positions of the most significant places in Europe.' Until recently it had mainly been the big German cities, rivers and mountains, as well as European capitals, that the violent teacher had introduced his students to, but as the war got under way more and more unknown names were added, places where the armed forces had won victories and where German bombs had left everything in ashes and ruins. Every German victory was drummed into the children with vicious blows if they could not instantly locate the position on the map. He was, however, not the only flogging pedagogue in the school. Blows, raps with sticks on the knuckles, back and buttocks, as well as other forms of corporal punishment, were seen as natural and daily methods of educational discipline.

We were still too young to participate, so all that was left for us was to watch this Polish campaign from the cinema seat. We saw on the screen how 'our men' in a hail of bullets fearlessly stormed enemy nests and we saw how fast the Polish *soldateska* escaped. We knew the Polish seasonal workers [who now would have been in the defending army] better than most because during the harvest each year they used to cross the border to the eastern German provinces in order to earn some good German *Reichmark*. To us they were simple, callous, illiterate Poles, primitive people who were fit only for doing dirty work. 'Polish' was equivalent to scum, something uncouth, uneducated and uncivilised. That was what we were told, that the Poles were sub-human, a people born to be submissive.

Shit! Fighting was going on everywhere, but we were too young for the baptism of fire that changes boys to real men. The soldiers on leave were admired from all sides. Their stories of adventure from the centre of world history could open the strongest hearts of young girls at the time, but we who were born too late just had to stay on the side-lines and watch. Clearly we were envious and wanted to have a part in this war adventure; we wanted to be at the centre of glory, grasping the limelight.

Chapter 8

Helping Hitler Save the World

In April 1942, Peter Schilling voluntarily joined the heavy motorised artillery in Frankfurt-on-Oder. 'Otherwise I would have been drafted six months later, but I didn't want to wait any longer. At last I could become a hero myself.'

The young man's soul had been filled by a potent patriotism, but it would not be long before that would go. His officers quickly destroyed the idealistic youthful enthusiasm. The training was hard and the harassment during the time as a recruit went beyond anything that the young man could ever have imagined. Peter was not surprised that the training was tough – he had fully expected that; after all, they were to be prepared for front-line duties. But what was impossible for him to understand was the need for the never-ending harassment that he and his fellow recruits were exposed to from the boot camp sergeants.

Reasons for punishing the recruits were easily found or invented, and these punishments were sadistic and brutal. Senior officers looked the other way but, of course, they knew what was going on; they were all part of it. The 'training' methods were, as with most boot camps, approved and authorised from the very top of the hierarchy.

> Ever after, I have felt a deep aversion as soon as I hear Frankfurt an der Oder mentioned, the city that was the site for this training. I feel disgust and aggression. I cannot remember all the details; I cannot remember any names of these people. We just hated them so much, those we were totally in the hands of. We swore we would kill them from behind as soon as we got to the front.

But nothing would come from that promise. Very rarely these sergeants followed their recruits to the front – due to concerns about their own safety. What Peter most of all learned from this time on the banks of the River Oder was that the two concepts of 'being a soldier' and 'having a reflective mind' were totally incompatible. He also learned:

> The most important rule for warlords and officers is not to give their soldiers time to think or come to terms with their experiences. When soldiers start to think, their fighting morale becomes lax and their conviction about the rightfulness of their actions starts to disintegrate.

Peter Schilling.

After three months' recruit training Peter was deployed for service with the Third Reich's armed forces. Here the young man's view of the world would change even more. The glorious heroic war would soon lose its glory, and he would see very little of the anticipated heroism. In addition, even the propaganda picture of the 'sworn enemies' that until now he had so willingly accepted would have to be revised and questioned, after having met them himself.

Peter's experiences were many, but to me a few fairly surreal episodes stand out. One of them was a late evening rendezvous with the enemy at a Belgrade public house. The young man, now stationed in the occupied Serbian capital, had an evening off and, all on his own – which he preferred, as he wanted to meet the locals – he had entered an off-the-beaten-track bar. For a young German soldier who was part of unwelcome occupation forces this was indeed a singularly bad idea. In the bar Peter found himself surrounded by Partisans. Not surprisingly, they found the naïve German youngster interesting. Peter quickly told them the truth: he was unarmed, and had not come to fight but to have a drink or two. Still, there was no question that, on his own here and a member of Hitler's *Wehrmacht*, he was in serious personal danger. They could easily let him 'disappear', and this he was told. It was true that in this part of Belgrade the Partisans were more powerful than the German army, and alone he would stand no chance.

'But why would you do that?' was his innocent response. 'When we talk nicely to each other, why would you kill me?' The leader of the Partisan group was astonished, and they all laughed after he had said something to the others. As Peter had then asked why they hated the Germans so much, they obviously must have found him completely comical. Indeed, they were flabbergasted, but luckily for him, they listened to what he had to say. So, with great confidence, the *Wehrmacht* private, surrounded by Partisans in a Belgrade bar, then started to 'preach': 'You must be grateful; we have saved you from civil war and internal violence. Germany only wants to bring peace and unity to Europe.' And he went on in that manner. Peter spoke convincingly, at least so he thought. He repeated all the propaganda lies he had been fed himself. In hindsight, however, the Partisans obviously found it all rather pathetic or maybe even farcical and entertaining. In fact, as he remembered it, they even wanted more: 'When I stopped in my flow of words a few times, they asked me to continue.'

However, after a while, when he finally had had enough, the leader started to speak, and Peter now got to hear another version than the one he had been fed by Goebbels. The Partisan commander proclaimed:

> Prince Paul has betrayed Yugoslavia to the Germans. He invited the Germans, as he was obviously afraid the Russians would come. Now the Croatians have chosen to side with the Germans and Serbs are being deported; whole families had to quickly pack whatever few belongings they could bring with them. Helped by the Germans and under death threats, the Serbs were forced out of their homes and evicted from their native land. The Germans rob the country, and if anybody dares to protest they are shot. But the Serbs love their freedom and will fight back. They will not let themselves be kicked out by the Germans, or the Croats and their Ustascha.

Peter got a lesson in politics; he was told about the shortage of almost everything, and about the suffering, plundering and killing of whole families.

> I couldn't believe it, but it was probably safest to say I could understand. It was dark when I left. The Partisan leader assigned me two of his men as guards that night; they took me back safely to my camp.

This rendezvous with the enemy sowed the first doubts in the young soldier's mind. What was actually going on? For him this was the beginning of a long and very painful lesson in extreme human cruelty. Much more was to come. As his unit continued down to Greece, he would see it all with his own eyes: there was no more a need to be told of reality in a Belgrade bar.

Stalino

Donetsk is a city in the eastern part of Ukraine; during the Stalin era, and therefore at the time of the war, it was known as Stalino. This is where Peter Schilling's unit was stationed after having been transferred once more – from Greece to the likewise invaded Soviet Union. Again, it was what Peter would see and hear while on leave, not only on active duty, that would make him reflect on life.

So, what was there to do on a day off in the occupied Stalinist Stalino?

Not knowing what to do with my time, I walked aimlessly around, and all of a sudden I heard screams. Horrified people were driven out of their houses by soldiers and herded on to lorries with blows and kicks. There were men, women and children among them; there were old people and there were many very young. I saw a woman with a baby on her arm who was not fast enough getting up on the back of the lorry. She got a rifle-butt in her back and was screamed at to hurry up. Then suddenly a soldier whipped the child out of her arms and threw it into the dark room of the carriage. Another woman was beaten by a soldier with the butt of his rifle and as she helplessly crawled aboard the lorry, the fullness of her stomach disclosed that she was pregnant.

Pte Schilling was upset by what he saw and approached one of the guards.

'This is unbelievable! Who is responsible for this outrage?'

'Mind your own bloody business. These are Jews and other scum; they must get out of here.'

'The indifference and irresponsibility shown by a large part of the general population have contributed considerably to the inhumanity that is taking place. Who, for example, protested when they first started to go for the Communists, then for the Jews, then for the disabled? All the time people were thinking: "Well, it's not about me; I am not affected." But the truth is: What is right cannot be divided, so when someone passively watches when someone else puffs to the breeze, he cannot be surprised and claim innocence when next day there is a storm all around us. Somehow there is a concatenation of sins. Nobody can say: "I am totally innocent." And most sins are sins of omission. The years of inhumanity are just so inhuman because so many have taken part. Also the churches are guilty; they sold Christianity so cheap, and still they call themselves Christians. In reality they are only Christians by name.'

François de Beaulien in 1943

(Because of his letters to his mother, he was sentenced to prison for *Wehrkraftzersetzung*)

'We must not take prisoners!' was a frequently heard instruction that, if one did not know better, sounded fairly innocent. One day it became clear to Peter what this instruction in reality meant:

One morning two defectors from the enemy side were reported. They had successfully sneaked into our camp during the night and had surrendered to our forces. A corporal then took them to the headquarters of the battalion where they were quickly interrogated. After that the non-commissioned officer was ordered to take them away and shoot them. They got a bullet in the neck and it was fast and painless, but … it was blatant murder! They had had no weapons; they didn't want to shoot at us and they had

given themselves up voluntarily, as they were fed up with their own dictator, Stalin.
You cannot just shoot people like that as if they were vermin.

One reason for not taking prisoners was that there was no place for them; moreover, there were no transport facilities, not enough provisions, and no guards available to keep an eye on them. At least, so it was said. For Peter this would soon present him with a conundrum of his own.

The troops to which he belonged had again been moved. They now found themselves on the Kalmyk Steppe. The plan was to attack a town called Atschikulak, and this attack was to become the young man's baptism of fire. The attack followed, and it was here for the first time, but far from the last, that Peter saw mortally wounded and dead soldiers lying in grotesque postures. As he talked about it years later, he could not remember all the horrible details; he must have repressed much of it in order to be able to carry on with life. But after Atschikulak had been taken, there were to be numerous similar episodes of killing and maiming; this way of life was to become 'normal'.

'Often it is said that a baptism of fire changes a boy into a man. But what a lie,' an old man said years later, as he talked about the events that had ruined so many years of his youth. 'What it did was to destroy a man's sense of decency and humanity.' Peter had seen all his dead comrades lying there; but after a few hours they were all just forgotten, never talked about again. Nothing more was said about their pain, screams and horrible wounds. Not a word more about spouting arteries, fear and horror, or, for that matter, the staring eyes of the dead. It was all 'forgotten'. With the help of vodka it was suppressed.

How else could one control the tremble in the legs? How else could we have tried to survive another day ourselves? No, there was no time to think about those who were no longer with us; it was as if they had never existed.

Our camp was like a small island on the huge Russian steppe. The next village was probably twenty or thirty kilometres away; there was no real front line. Sometimes Russian soldiers on horses could be seen out there. But from our position it was difficult to know in which villages their soldiers might be stationed. It was all like a Wild West game, like cowboys and Indians. Sometimes they were there, sometimes somewhere else, or so it seemed from a distance. Also our unit started to patrol the area on horses. I volunteered as I knew how to ride. But to be out there on horseback was extremely dangerous. Occasionally the Soviet air forces would turn up, and a riding soldier would have made an easy target for those pilots.

It was in this situation that the old instruction 'We must not take prisoners' came back into his mind. What if a runaway Soviet soldier, a deserter, reported to him? One day the horrible scenario nearly came true. Near the camp were a few abandoned houses and farm buildings and in there a few hens and other animals had been left behind. On and off, German soldiers went there to supplement their meat rations, and Peter had been part of that as well.

One day he went on his own. It had appeared safe, as there had been no signs of Soviet patrols in the area for quite a few days. With his carbine under his arm, ready to shoot what he could find, he walked in between the houses and around a corner. Then, all of a sudden, he stood face to face with a Soviet soldier with a machine gun. It was as if the other guy had been out on the same job.

I froze; we stared at each other and then the Red Army service man smiled, lowered his gun, and started to walk slowly towards me.

'I saw you coming,' he said in understandable German; 'would you like to defect to us?' The Russian seated himself on a bench and put his weapon away. Warily I walked over and sat down beside him doing the same. 'Shall I give myself up or will you?' he asked. 'Don't do it,' I said. 'A few days ago some of your friends did and they were killed with a shot in the neck.' He looked at me; he couldn't understand. 'We wouldn't do that,' he said. After that he suggested that I should come with him. I could even return and ask some of my friends to join me, he suggested. 'Then we would come and pick you up here.'

But Pte Schilling shook his head. As he explained all those years later about this most remarkable rendezvous between two young men on a Russian steppe right in the middle of the Second World War, no, he could not do that, he could not leave all his friends behind. After all, they were facing the same threats, dangers and difficulties; he could not just leave them.

Peter never told anybody about this meeting on his return to camp. But the memory of it stayed with him for the rest of his life, the memory of a most extraordinary encounter. Unfortunately he could not allow himself to return the Russian soldier's offer. He knew how that would have ended.

Chapter 9

Having Learned the Truth

I had willingly and voluntarily joined the armed forces convinced that the world would be healed by listening to the German soul. I then learned that this German soul was not separate from starving people in Greece, suppressed people in Yugoslavia, ill-treated and deported women and children in Stalino, and murdered prisoners of war in Atschikulak. The German soul was also a screaming Goebbels and his hysterical crowds of supporters. Now I had to think everything through from scratch. Yet to think as a soldier was dangerous and troublesome. With mindfulness it begins and one never knows where it will end. My friend Heinz had sowed a seed that left me no rest. 'Honestly, we should do something about it,' he said. 'Yes, we have to!' The thought kept going round and round in my head. It's the same if one actively participates in a horrific deed or passively watches it take place, isn't it?

Next came three days' funeral leave. Now the focal point of young Peter's life was gone: his mother had suddenly died in childbirth. The funeral was to be joined by the christening of his little newborn sister. So there he stood by his mother's coffin with the little baby in his arms, fighting off the heretical thought that would not leave his head, no matter how hard he tried:

What a horrible teaching that spreads the message that unless a newborn innocent child has been christened or baptised, he or she, in case of death, will be denied entrance to heaven – no matter whether it was on the door of the Protestant or Catholic version he or she had knocked. For that reason only, it had to be quick; for that reason this little child's christening had to coincide with her own mother's sad funeral – and all this right in the middle of a genocidal war.

Peter was happy to leave as soon as the services were over. After this experience he hated this place even more. The time was moving nearer; he now had to make plans for his own life, disregarding what plans the Führer might have had for him:

It's difficult to know if I would have made a different decision had my mother not died. At least I know that it was clear to me that now I did not have to worry about her. I could no longer do her any harm. That had always been the touchstone for me, no matter what I had been up to in life. Now I could justify myself faster and more easily.

Dead people do not need any explanation; they cannot oppose or criticise you. They can neither give their approval, nor shake their heads in dismay.

More than anything else, Peter had found one simple sentence that answered all the questions he had asked himself lately. In an illegal Marxist book he had read that 'the only fair and just war is a people's war against its own oppressors'. Now he knew what he needed to do. On his own he had to take up his fight, the fight against the Nazis and their cohorts. In the Balkans and in Russia he had seen and heard things that made him think, things which had opened his eyes to what was going on. As he returned on leave he saw more and more of the same in Germany itself. He started to see things that before he had not been prepared to realise were there.

'Why hadn't I seen it all before? After all, it was all so obvious what was going on. Why had I been blind to it?' Yes, why had he? As he said, years after, it was not just the infamous Jewish yellow star that signalled a new perception all over the country of some fellow German compatriots. They were not the only ones Aryans should stay away from. Polish forced workers had to wear a 'P' to distinguish themselves from 'normal' people. As with the yellow star, those wearing a 'P' on their chest were sub-human. With all such people, 'real' Germans were not allowed to mingle. He had heard it before, back in his childhood, but here it was even worse, and it was meant very seriously: 'If you touch dirt you get dirty.' In fact, personal contact with such people was seen as a criminal offence. In the newspapers one could read about those dishonourable creatures who had crossed this line of 'honourable conduct' and dirtied themselves by interacting with the untouchable. If caught, the punishment was severe.

Of course, under such circumstances it was not easy for a young man who had been brought up to be obedient to authorities to make up his own mind and go his own way. And these issues could not be addressed in the community; any attempt would be met by silence, and it could be very dangerous: the risk of being reported was huge. In the family circle it was also like that.

Peter's uncle Fritz was a vicar but also captain of the reserves. He fulfilled a dual role; he served in the army but had also been given time to look after his parish. The young nephew visited the clergyman/captain whenever he could. So it had been before the war, and so it had remained. That is until this special day when Peter visited his uncle to ask him for a profound and serious conversation. 'Our relationship was very good. I had trust in this uncle. And therefore, shortly after the death of my mother, I asked him for a personal talk.'

As the two men sat in the vicarage study, Peter – fully trusting that his uncle would be the right person to unburden his worries to and seek advice from – started to talk about all his recent experiences. He talked about his unhappiness with the war and with what was going on around him, both at home and abroad. And he was honest; he talked about the utter disgust he often felt:

I find it's all shameful for Germany and for the German cause. And we are sent to fight for such revolting crap. One has to do something about it. Would you, Uncle Fritz, bring it up here and in the army?

His uncle's expression became more and more icy. Suddenly Fritz got to his feet and put on his uniform jacket with his rank as captain.

> Enraged, he just stared at me, and then: 'Private Schilling,' his scathing voice spoke, 'I have never heard such defeatist talk before. I never want to hear it again. Never! Understood? Never again in my house and never anywhere else! Remember your oath! What you are saying is complete nonsense; it is close to treason! You could be court-martialled! I tell you, only because I think of your mother,' his voice got softer, 'I will not take this any further. Only for her I will not throw you out of this house immediately. Have you understood? Never talk such nonsense anymore.'

Peter would never forget this discussion with his uncle. But he never visited him again – not during the war, not after. If this man's words did anything to the youngster it was to further establish him in his conviction that he could be part of this crime no more. He felt disgust and shame. After all, he was still a small cog in the machinery of death and destruction. No, he no longer wanted to identify himself with the German people of whom this uncle was an example. From now on he became a radical opponent in his mind – and soon also in action.

> After having listened to Uncle Fritz, I saw everything much more sharply. Now suddenly it was clear to me: of course, the Führer also knows it all. He also knows what is going on. People know; it's not just me who does.

Peter began to remember talks he had overheard in the past, between his father and others.

> Of course they had known much more than as a youngster I had. After all, the yellow star, the 'P', it was all a part of the country's legislation. What I had seen as a child, what I had found uninteresting and unimportant, all of that suddenly came into another light. Of course, it was all connected … and they knew. No, with such disgrace I would have to dissociate myself.

The escape started from Bahnhof Zoo railway station in Berlin. It was to be a nerve-racking journey in an overcrowded carriage. In a way, as he later recalled, the crowd protected him from the frequent controls and identity checks, and eventually, miraculously, he reached his final destination close to the Swiss border without having been discovered. From there he sneaked his way into the forest in order to make the last part of the escape across the border.

Over the Swiss border

Having safely crossed the border into Switzerland, Peter Schilling walked on in search of further protection and help. After a while he was successful, found a farmhouse and was welcomed in. The evening meal was just being served; the family did not ask many questions but just looked at his face and uniform and understood – one more plate was put on the table. Mashed potatoes and apples. It was a heavenly meal.

The next day, the refugee found himself in a Swiss railway carriage, escorted by a distrustful military policeman. However, after the officer had convinced himself of the benign nature of the German deserter and noted that there was no immediate risk of escape, he changed his grimace, relaxed and enjoyed the journey through the autumn landscape.

Peter recalled:

He didn't speak much, but the war, the front, the bombing campaigns against the German cities, all that captured his interest. His horizons, however, didn't reach further than the cantonal boundaries, and for Hitler and the German war campaign he had unlimited respect. Through his questions he again and again made it clear that he had no understanding whatsoever of why a soldier would escape his duties. 'An oath is an oath and the Bolsheviks have to be kept down. What would become of Switzerland if all Germans suddenly escaped from Hitler?' I ignored his bigotry. In the newspapers and on the radio he could, if he had been interested, have had sufficient information about what was going on. I couldn't help him.

'Germany defends Europe against the Communists and in doing so it defends the interests of the freedom-loving Swiss,' he continued. 'How can we tolerate all these foreigners who are pouring into our country? What are we to do with all these refugees and deserters?' This arrival of bogus asylum seekers was a threat to the security of Switzerland, and the Swiss had to pay benefits to these people who were a burden to each and every taxpayer, I was told. 'Switzerland is no place for these strangers and there is not enough work here. An oath that is sworn to the Lord keeps its validity at all times and under all circumstances.'

It later dawned on Peter that this view was not unusual in Switzerland, and that he just could not understand. He could not understand how they could think in such a way in this country that was supposed to be the oldest Middle-European democracy. But, as he said a bit cynically, maybe it was he who was mistaken; maybe it was he who was wrong. Perhaps all the others were sound and healthy in their views and thought clearly.

Witzwil was the name of their destination, he had been told – a refugee camp. When they arrived, however, it was very different from what Peter had expected. It was a prison. Soon after arrival, after he had had his hair cut to the length of half a matchstick, he was put in a tiny cell in the upper tier. Peter had reached freedom; he had escaped Hitler. Though he had been locked up, he still felt freer than he had for a very long time:

That day in my solitude I came to the conclusion that there is no greater contradiction than the claim that military discipline is necessary for the defence of individual freedom. There is nowhere, not even in this prison cell, where a human being is further away from his deep connection to other people, to his loved ones and friends than in enforced military service. Nowhere else is he more enslaved and nowhere else is it more difficult for him to be in touch with his emotions. Nevertheless, it is said that military duty is necessary in order to protect one's freedom, family, people and Fatherland. Isn't it a lie? All those who had to participate in this war will have to carry with them for ever its cruelty and will always remain its victims. It sticks to us like a burning Nessus shirt from which we can never be free. War was a great source of suffering for all of our generation, and each of us has had to carry it with us to the end of life.

The admission process of the prison quickly reduced Peter to a number, and the clothes he was made to wear – a grey uniform and cap with heavy shoes which allowed only a slow, shuffling walk – completed the picture. True, after a few days he was transferred to a sort of refugee camp, but this camp was part of the same prison and in a way it was all the same.

> From now on we were nobodies and were treated as such. We no longer belonged to the human race or to society. In the refugee camp part of the penitentiary there were around 130-140 Italian and German prisoners. We were held in three big dormitories, but apart from that, the conditions were the same as for everybody else.

Very soon refugee Schilling's initial sense of moral superiority in relation to those sent here to serve sentences for committed crimes completely disappeared. After all, they were all in this together, no matter what had brought them there. And it was not as if the refugee population made the stay any safer for a German war defector. No, it was not only wise to stay clear of the deputy warden, who would use any opportunity to mete out sadistic punishments; for a German deserter it was also of paramount importance to stay clear of many of his compatriots. Numerous German nationals with Swiss residency had been locked up there as a national precaution. These people would have been more than happy to beat up a guy like Peter, had they got the chance.

Chapter 10

Escape to Sweden

As a neutral country at the heart of continental Europe, Switzerland was an obvious destination for German war refugees of any kind, not only deserters. As there were not many alternatives this was true, even if the Alpine republic's refugee laws were extremely strict and did not even allow asylum status to be granted on the basis of race or ethnicity – not least endangering Jews fleeing the Holocaust. That the country managed to remain free of Nazi occupation was due to a multitude of reasons, but one of them was definitely its convenience as a neutral business partner, making it possible for Germany to import indispensable commodities from other countries. Gold and other valuables stolen from Holocaust victims would have played an important role in these transactions, but, as it all helped Switzerland to stay 'neutral', this moral dilemma was taken as part of the bargain.

Another of the very few options available to a potential German deserter was Sweden, my homeland. Like Switzerland, Sweden was 'neutral' and stayed unoccupied throughout the war. But, unfortunately, neither of these two countries would become an unwavering protector of anybody fleeing Hitler. The Swiss, as we have just seen, did not welcome deserters (or others, for that matter) with open arms, and it was not easy to get there. When it came to Sweden it was very much the same, though, apart from the borders with Finland and Norway and the Öresund crossing from Denmark, to get there could be a fair bit easier – all due to the transit trains.

After the German occupation of Norway, Sweden entered into an agreement with Nazi Germany to allow the *Wehrmacht* the use of Swedish railways for the transport of goods and troops to and from its occupied Nordic neighbour. This was the price that the Swedish authorities had been happy to pay in order to remain free themselves. It was from these trains that fleeing German soldiers jumped.

After the war a Swedish state commission, the Sandler Commission, was assigned to look into what had happened to these and other war refugees. Their final report, *SOU 1946:36 Betänkande angående flyktingars behandling* (Report on the Treatment of Refugees), does not make comfortable reading. It reveals that a secret regulation regarding refugees was introduced on 1 November 1940 by State Secretary Tage Erlander.

At the time that Erlander signed this document, he was in charge of all the country's internment camps. What Erlander – who after the war went on to serve as Social Democratic Prime Minister for a record twenty-three uninterrupted years – had signed and kept secret from his fellow Swedes (though it would most likely have made no difference had he told them) was an instruction declaring that 'German deserters must be returned to their homeland, as they are not to be seen as political refugees'. The message to the law enforcers was clear: 'People belonging to the German armed forces who have absconded from service and arrived in the country shall be returned immediately.'

To the best of my knowledge, there was an agreement with the German authorities that Sweden would send these defectors back. The reason was obvious: the Swedish government was keen not to provoke Hitler. If it were to be known that a deserter could enjoy protection, more soldiers would defect from the trains. The number of defectors might explode, it was feared, and very probably this would have been proved right had precautions not been taken. The low number of defections in the early war years was probably down to the unambiguous information German soldiers were given by their officers: 'Desertion on your way through Sweden will lead to your certain death. You will be sent back to face the consequences.' As we have seen, it was no empty threat. The Swedes would help to assure that.

Apart from those who still jumped off the trains, many escaped over the borders with Finland and Norway. At least fifteen of those deserters were sent back to Norway by Swedish authorities. According to available information, these people were all sentenced to death by German war courts and executed. But it is very likely that the actual number is much higher.

However, happily, some deserters, despite what has been written so far, were actually allowed to stay. After 1942 – when German fortunes started to turn – the rules were changed and the deportations stopped. These people would from then on be held in a number of camps in which political opponents of the German regime as well as Jewish refugees were interned. Examples of those camps are Långmora, Smedsbo, Rinkaby and Vägershult. In the latter a total of 350 German deserters were held.

They were now safe from the German military courts, but if the war refugees, whether military or civilian, thought they had come to heaven they were to be disappointed. Refugees from Germany, and I am not talking only about defectors from the armed forces, were not welcomed with open arms in Sweden, and some of these camps were later called by Swedish researchers 'concentration camps in the shadow of the Third Reich'. In these camps, prisoners had no right to challenge their captivity and they would not even be told why they had been deprived of their freedom.

Swedish sympathy with Nazi Germany was widespread and went all the way to the top of society. The following story – presented in an old copy of my childhood local newspaper *Barometern* – might help clarify what kind of 'neutral' state it was that returned German deserters to most certain death. It was the summer of 1941 and the attack on the Soviet Union, Operation Barbarossa, was under way. On 9 July troop-carrying German ships sailed past the Swedish island Öland on their way to Leningrad. By doing so they must have come slightly off course and were heading dangerously close to mined Swedish waters. Seeing what was about to happen, the Swedish navy sent warnings in an attempt to make the German vessels change course.

I do not in any way defend the mining of waters in order to kill sailors, in this case mainly conscripts, but I wonder why the mines had been put out there in the first place, if, as it seems, as soon as foreign naval vessels came close to being in harm's way, Swedish authorities went to great efforts to warn them. Was it all down to the nationality of the ships in question? Whose ships would they have been happy to see blown up?

No matter, the Germans obviously did not take the warnings seriously and continued full speed ahead right into the minefield with catastrophic consequences and many deaths. Survivors of the explosions were rescued by the Swedish navy, and I am happy about that. But what strikes me further about this case is that only a month after the event – which, after all, had been caused by mines which had been deliberately laid – a joint German-Swedish commemorative ceremony took place in the little village of Össby at the southern tip of Öland.

It was quite a remarkable situation: German deserters were still being sent back to face Nazi war justice, all in line with Erlander's instructions; only a short distance away Hitler's forces were in the process of brutally invading the neighbouring Soviet Union; yet here, in a 'neutral' country, as if we were all among dear friends, a memorial for the deceased was to be unveiled. It was a joint ceremony attended by representatives of both countries' armed forces, the German consul and Swedish dignitaries such as the future Crown Prince and his wife (both with well-known sympathies for the southern neighbour). In his speech the Swedish royal – the present king's father who was later killed in an air crash and therefore never came to the throne himself – said: 'These men have sacrificed their lives fighting for their homeland. Remember to do the same if asked to.'

As a final honour on a fine day, Swedish soldiers fired a salute, the German consul gave the 'Heil Hitler' greeting, with the royal couple to his left, and, astonishingly, the Swedish army orchestra played Horst Wessel's Song – the official anthem of the Nazi party. The guests would have used the original German text, but this is a translation of what was sung on a sunny day at the southern tip of Öland at the height of the Second World War:

> This is the final
> Bugle call to arms.
> Already we are set
> Prepared to fight.
> Soon Hitler's flags will wave
> O'er every single street.
> Enslavement ends
> When soon we set things right.

As we have heard, after the initial German success was turned into a looming defeat in the war, largely as a result of the failure of the attack of which this event had been a small part, Sweden, sitting on the fence, also changed its rules to accommodate new circumstances. Accordingly, from November 1942 no extraditions of deserters took place.

One of those who benefited from that change of attitude was Herbert Bartholmes. In March 1943, the twenty-year-old had jumped from a transit train passing Öxnered. Herbert returned to Germany after the war and was part of the development of the Free German Youth (FDJ), the official Communist youth movement in the Soviet occupied zone. However, disillusioned by what he experienced there, he returned to Sweden in 1954 – while it was still possible to get out of the young 'Democratic' Republic of Germany – and ended up as a teacher in Vänersborg. Young Herbert had had luck in a hard time. True, as he jumped from the train he hurt his leg and was left with a limp for the rest of his life, but, as we have seen, not all of his fellow compatriots trying Sweden as an escape route had been as fortunate.

When looking back to those days, we have to remember that 'neutral' Sweden was a country with a great ability to adapt to whoever was ruling or was about to rule the world. Fortunately that was to change, though it would take some time. After Erlander had been replaced by Olof Palme as Prime Minister, another view on deserters – this time, Americans escaping yet another war crime, Vietnam – was introduced. Criticising a superpower's aggressive behaviour against a small country a world away, while welcoming the aggressor's defecting soldiers, was not popular and might even have led to his subsequent assassination, but, from this book's point of view, it was a far more honourable act than the appeasement regulation issued by his predecessor.

Chapter 11

Young Resistance

It might not be well known, but it was not only Peter Schilling who found out what the war was all about; he was not the only young person who made up his mind. There were others who did as well, in one way or another. Certainly, not all German youngsters allowed themselves to be abused and misled. Youthful opposition to the Nazi regime could be found in many shapes and forms: it could be refusal to join the Hitler Youth or the League of German Girls; it could be refusal to greet with the Nazi salute; it could be to help people 'who should not be helped'; or it could be much more.

Rebellious behaviour was common among members of groups like the *Edelweißpiraten* (Edelweiss Pirates) and *Swingjugend* (Swing Kids). These loosely organised groups were basically apolitical. Looking back, we might see them as examples of young people's counter-cultures, something that can be found in all societies at all times. But these groups were definitely anti-Nazi. They were a reaction against the Nazi ideology, and, not least, they opposed the strict regimentation of young people's lives that came with the new rulers. More political and better organised was another youth group, *Leipzig Meuten* (the Leipzig Packs). They based their opposition to the Nazis on their own socialist ideology. But common to all these groups was strong opposition to the Hitler regime and attempts to evade everything that came with it, including conscription. As young people in all countries at all times, they wanted to go their own way and make up their own mind. While the big cities of Hamburg and Berlin were centres for the *Swingjugend*, the *Edelweißpiraten* were found mainly in the state of Saxony and in the Ruhr district, and, as the name implies, the *Meuten* were from Leipzig.

A smaller but very well organised group was the *Weiße Rose* (White Rose). This group was founded by students in Munich. Leading members were the siblings Hans and Sophie Scholl, Christoph Probst, Willi Graf and Alexander Schmorell. After their arrest in 1943, they were sentenced to death for *Wehrkraftzersetzung*, 'assisting the enemy' and 'preparing for treason' by the infamous chief judge of the People's Court, Roland Freisler. The courage shown by many of these young people in such difficult times was extraordinary, and, as happened to the members of the *Weiße Rose*, they often paid with their lives.

The number of young opponents increased and the extent of rebellious behaviour accelerated the longer the war carried on. In response to this growing resistance, the Nazi machinery reacted with a dramatic increase in the number of arrests and by building concentration camps for young people (*Jugendschutzlager* –Youth

Roland Freisler, the notorious chief judge of the People's Court.

'Protection' Camps). Camp Moringen near Göttingen was an example of such a camp. Here young people were locked up for not toeing the adult world's line – that of the Nazis.

Apart from all these more or less organised groups there were young people who showed their distaste in their own way as best they could. All these young people's activities were part of the resistance that *did* exist. However, we must not forget that it was the armed forces that paved the way and made the Holocaust possible. Therefore, refusal of war service was the most powerful instrument a young person could use. Unfortunately, in doing so it would very often mean death at a time when life had only just started.

A radical act

Whether young or a little bit older, desertion was the ordinary man's way of showing resistance – resistance to a war he found to be criminal, or just resistance to a life he had never chosen and did not want. It would certainly not be correct to claim that all German troop deserters during the Second World War were deeply convinced resistance fighters and anti-Fascist heroes, and that is in no way the intention of this book. The intention is rather to claim that every human being has, or at least should have, a right to his own life and a fundamental right not to be forced to kill and maim others. Or, as Peter Schilling writes in his 'Deserter's Song', printed at the end of this book: 'I won't let you dictate to me; if I need a foe, I will find him myself.'

So who were the deserters and what motives did they have? To such a question we are able only to say that for obvious reasons it will never be possible to find out precisely what caused each and every individual to take the decision he took. So many years have now passed, and as only a few of those who survived the war ever spoke about it (all this due to the extreme hostility shown to them in post-war society) and now no longer can be asked, we can only guess as to the specific motives they all had. Still, looking at what *is* known and what we *can* read in documents and letters, it is possible to form an idea.

Jehovah's Witness Friedrich Bicker was married, had one son and lived in Dortmund-Mengede. He remained active in the church even after it had been forbidden by the Nazis, and despite being arrested and tortured by the Gestapo. From early 1936 to late 1937, he was imprisoned in Dortmund and Bochum. In 1942, Bicker was drafted into the army and did not refuse – as many other Jehovah's Witnesses did. However, after being ordered to be part of a firing squad, he handed in a written statement in which he refused further service. As a consequence, he was sentenced to death for *Wehrkraftzersetzung* on 28 April 1944 and beheaded in Roter Ochse prison in Halle three weeks later.

Religious doubt about the righteousness of warfare in general and this conflict in particular would definitely have haunted many a soldier and helped push him over the edge. On a daily basis to be exposed to harsh and brutal military discipline would have been another reason, and that, combined with horrendous experiences at the front, could easily have finished off even the strongest mind and soul. Soldiers who experience the most gruesome side of war often go through a personality change. In particular, among those serving under the Nazis, this increased awareness would have changed the attitudes of some who initially might have had a supportive or indifferent approach to the war and made them into active opponents of it.

We must also not forget those who saw desertion as the only opportunity to escape death, those who simply tried to save their own lives, or those who were terrified at the thought of having to participate in the madness of mass slaughter and destruction. It is essential to be aware of this persistent fear of death that the soldiers had to endure. Whatever the reason, which of us, who were not there, has a right to pass judgement on those who were – though they had never asked for it? After all, most of these people, whether they defected or not, were just victims of a war on which they had had no say.

But there were also definitely many young people about whom there can be no question of how to describe them. They were heroes, and Stefan Hampel was one of the greatest. In May 1942, he witnessed mass shootings of Jews by an *SS Einsatzgruppe* (mobile death squad) – an experience that led him to desert from the army.

Stefan Hampel.

Hampel burned his uniform in Grodno and joined a Polish resistance group in Lithuania. After a year there he decided the world needed to know what was happening to the Jewish population in Eastern Europe and he left with the intention of making his way to inform the International Red Cross in Switzerland. Certainly, it was an extremely dangerous task he had taken on, and he did not make it all the way. He was arrested in Freiburg and sentenced to death for desertion on 11 August 1943. Fortunately, he was lucky: a plea for clemency was unexpectedly granted and he was transferred to a penal battalion. Hampel miraculously survived even that, and in the end also the war. But what he had done for humanity was never acknowledged during his lifetime: for the rest of his life he remained an outcast.

When in prison in Freiburg, he wrote:

In May 1942, I had been given leave from my unit that was located near Grodno, Lida and Wilna (in western Belarus). During this leave I experienced something that was to become the final reason for me to do what I finally did. In Wassiliski they hermetically cordoned off the ghetto and at an open place a gigantic grave was dug. Now all the Jews from the ghetto were rounded up, and I saw them being forced to walk towards the mass grave. Specifically old women and children were shot already while on their way to the grave. Afterwards the streets were littered with corpses. Before these around two thousand (as I later realised) Jews were forced to enter the grave, they were forced to strip to their underwear. Many mothers carried infants in their arms.

Beware of chained dogs

Just as there were many reasons for desertion, there were also many ways of disappearing. There were people who, encouraged by enemy propaganda, ran over to the other side to surrender and ask for protection. There were also soldiers who joined enemy units and fought against German troops or chose to fight on the side of Partisans. There were also those who fled from the front and hid in the forests, and those who found their way back home and hid with friends or family – anywhere, in fact, they could find refuge.

Encouragement from the enemy to swap sides was part of the psychological war. From the Soviet side, flyers were thrown from aeroplanes with the promise of 'life, good treatment and being sent home at the end of the war'. The Western Allies also used propaganda widely. Despite this, large-scale defections had taken place only very rarely before the Battle of Stalingrad, but that slaughter was a turning point, and the number of defectors increased significantly after the summer of 1943.

Defecting to the enemy was not without considerable danger. Stories from defectors tell us how dangerous it was to change sides or even to think about it. The risk of being informed upon by comrades and landing in front of a war tribunal was a grim reality. One could also easily have been shot down while fleeing, by one's own troops or by the enemy. Many chose another way and escaped back to their native place and then went underground. This step into an illegal existence was fraught with great personal danger. Everywhere the *Kettenhunde* ('chained dogs') were hunting for their prey, and these notorious informers were more than happy to hand over a runaway soldier to the eagerly waiting war courts.

The precise time for desertion was seldom planned; it was most likely to take place when an opportune moment arrived, such as at the end of basic training, or the movement of troops to the front or some far-flung place. The desertion of friends or acquaintances might trigger it, or one could simply lose contact with one's comrades and be unable – or unwilling – to find one's way back. Or, as was often the case, a soldier might desert while on home leave.

After he was injured in Russia, Pte Gerhard Fritsche was allowed home on sick leave in 1943. 'At that time, father told me about what they did with the Jews, and then it was finished for me, over, final! I did not want to go back again.' The nineteen year old had had enough of the war and went into hiding with a girlfriend in Berlin. The military police found and arrested him, and he was taken to a war court and sentenced to death for deserting. Fritsche's hands were being tied to the execution post just as a message reached him that he had been pardoned. Nine others had just been shot.

Deliberate self-mutilation in order to avoid service was relatively rare. More often illness, the symptoms of which could be actively exacerbated, was a welcome respite from the front, leading to sanctuary in the infirmary. A period of leave following rehabilitation could be an ideal occasion for desertion. Faking symptoms, however, could be extremely dangerous; if detected, it could lead to prosecution and the looming likelihood of a death sentence.

The prospect of success as a fugitive in one's own country was dependent on numerous factors. Besides one's own personal ability to cope with such an extreme situation and the need for support from others, sheer luck played a major role. Generally, individual cases of desertion were not well planned and, in most cases, survival was organised only for the subsequent couple of weeks or maybe a month or two at best.

The sites used to hide deserters had to be changed regularly, both to avoid disclosure and because many makeshift hideouts were not suitable for a long stay, at least not in the winter months. Most were merely unheated huts in the mountains, a corner in a barn, a place in the forest or in a cave. It was not easy to stay for long under such circumstances. The main problem was getting and preparing food, as the deserters had to be cautious about firing hunting guns and lighting fires that would attract attention. This forced many to be extremely innovative. They had to learn quickly how to evaluate others and decide who they could trust and who they could not. If someone mistakenly believed a fellow human being could be relied on for help and support, the outcome could be fatal. And when being supported, there were serious logistical problems which needed to be faced. They had to arrange how to contact each other, where to deliver supplies, and how to overcome other practical problems.

Shortages would also lead to petty thefts, and this supported the theory and much-loved cliché of these runaways as criminals. During the war, negative images of the deserter as a common thief were widespread. These images were frequently used by some political groups, both after as well as during the war. But the fact that the perception of these men as common thieves was widespread cannot be explained purely by the wish to use smear tactics and false accusations against them; in fact, many, while being interrogated, willingly acknowledged such thefts in order to avoid informing on those who had helped them with food and other necessities.

Outside support was of vital importance, and the most significant support often came from their own families. It was not limited to material things; help was also needed if a deserter was taken ill or had to be warned of an imminent police raid. Moral support was vital to survival, as the deserter's isolation often created feelings of having done something wrong.

Anyone who belonged to the armed forces or was at risk of being drafted knew the dangers of not complying. The consequences were clear and unequivocal: 'He who does not follow orders to appear at his local draft board for conscription proceedings or he who ignores the draft by absenting himself or committing self-mutilation shall be punished by death.' In less serious cases, prison terms of up to ten years were considered. The same punishments were also meted out for conspirators and those who helped deserters in any way. The regime's attitude towards objectors knew no mercy, and those who helped them were treated in much the same way. In fact, simply being related to a deserter could lead to a person's arrest. Detention of family members happened frequently, and with this in mind, many potential deserters never even got as far as taking the final step; they did not wish to put their family in danger. Many who had deserted gave themselves up for the same reason.

Chapter 12

The Conspiracy

The first known assassination attempt on Hitler's life was by the Swabian carpenter Georg Elser from Heidenheim-on-Brenz. Elser acted alone without any connection to a resistance group. On 8 November 1939 he came as close to his goal as the more famous Col. Claus Schenk Graf von Stauffenberg did five years later.

Elser's intention was to kill the Führer with a time bomb, and he had carefully planned where it would be possible to execute his plan. Hitler was scheduled to speak at a beer hall, 'Bürgerbräukeller' at Rosenheimer Platz in Munich, and this would give Elser the chance to end the war by putting an end to the warmonger. Working secretly for over a month – at night, after successfully managing to remain undetected in the building after closing time – Elser hollowed out a pillar close to the rostrum from which the Chancellor was to speak. Here he would place the bomb that would kill the Führer and bring peace. Unfortunately, Elser's attempt to stop the war before it got going failed; he was arrested and spent the war years as a 'special security prisoner' in the concentration camps at Sachsenhausen and Dachau. On 9 April 1945, just before the end of the war, he was liquidated on Hitler's orders.

Others who were prepared to act were never able to get close enough to do so because of the tight security arrangements and Hitler's ever changing programme. Therefore, it was not until von Stauffenberg and the famous 20 July plot of 1944, which since the war has become synonymous with internal opposition to Hitler, that a major assassination attempt would again take place.

Apart from the people connected with Carl Friedrich Goerdeler, the former mayor of Leipzig, the most prominent civilian opponents of the Nazi dictatorship were concentrated around the Kreisau estate and its owner Helmuth Graf von Moltke. A number of people belonged to this group, which has become known as the *Kreisauer Kreis* (Kreisau Circle) – most of them conservatives from the traditional aristocracy, but others as well. They were united in their distaste for Nazism and constituted a sort of think-tank for a post-Hitler Germany. The group as such did not plan a coup. But, as we will see, others did, and some people from Kreisau would join those forces.

From the time that war was about to start, officers in the armed forces also began to have second thoughts about the future. It was not that they had any fundamental objections to the plans for German expansion, but they disapproved of technical details; they feared that the plan was premature and that the army needed more time

Georg Elser.

to prepare. Their worry was that if it was to go ahead as planned, it would end in a national catastrophe.

The unofficial head of this military opposition was Col. Gen. Ludwig Beck, the chief of the army general staff. As his warnings were ignored, he gave in his notice in August 1938, convinced that only the physical removal of the Nazi leader could save the nation from an impending disaster. Thereafter Beck became yet another person around whom people gathered. Among them were officers of the armed forces, diplomats, former politicians and union leaders. There would also have been contact with Goerdeler and people from the Kreisau Circle. This was the start of what has gone down in history as the conspiracy of 20 July 1944.

One of the officers who got involved in the planning of the assassination was Col. Claus Schenk Graf von Stauffenberg, who in the end would carry it out and whose name consequently became synonymous with the plot. In this context, however, it is important to note that though von Stauffenberg *had* been a member of the plotters and *did* carry it out, he was a latecomer. It was not until the later stages of the war that von Stauffenberg finally admitted the criminal character of Nazi politics and joined the resistance. Only slowly had he managed to free himself from the fascinating effect that Hitler's initial success and military victories had exerted over him. It is very likely that the unsuccessful development of the war contributed considerably to this change of position.

Von Stauffenberg, like most of his colleagues, was conservative in his political views. He came from a section of society where individuals were not only happy to support the ongoing 'national renewal of German life and state' but also wanted a final solution for what were termed 'social' problems. As a fervent patriot he had dedicated his life to the career of soldiering, so obedience and loyalty towards the leader of the state were for him – as for all his colleagues – an unquestionable matter of honour. And we know it remained so for years, both before and after the outbreak of war.

Then, after being severely injured – losing one eye, his right hand and the fingers of his left hand – von Stauffenberg was offered an important post immediately under Gen. Friedrich Olbricht, who for a long time had been a central power behind the military plans for a *coup d'état*. Olbricht now introduced von Stauffenberg to the plans and let him meet Beck. From his new central military position, von Stauffenberg thereafter tried to encourage the different opposition groups to work together. The message from now on was that Hitler must be killed, and, as von Stauffenberg put it, 'It is important to show both the German people as well as foreign countries that the German resistance has the courage to take this momentous step.'

After a number of unsuccessful attempts and the arrest of several influential members of the conspiracy, among them the evangelical priest Dietrich Bonhoeffer and his brother-in-law Hans von Dohnanyi, von Stauffenberg finally decided to carry out the plan himself. On 20 July 1944, he succeeded in smuggling a bomb into the Führer's heavily guarded and protected headquarters, 'Wolfsschanze' (Wolf's Lair), not far from the east Prussian town of Rastenburg (now Kętrzyn). Von Stauffenberg had access to the room where a meeting was to be held. He placed a briefcase with a time bomb underneath the table, close to the chair where Hitler was to sit – explaining before he left that he had to make a telephone call. The bomb detonated, but it was soon clear that Hitler had survived. Miraculously, he had been only slightly injured by

Col. Claus Schenk Graf von Stauffenberg, Admiral Karl-Jesco Otto von Puttkamer, Friedrich Fromm and Adolf Hitler at the Wolf's Lair.

the explosion, escaping with a damaged eardrum, burns to the left side of his body and a burned trouser leg.

The conspirators were quickly found and held to account. Von Stauffenberg, Olbricht and a few others were shot that same night in the courtyard at Bendlerblock in Berlin and, at his own request, Beck was given permission to commit suicide. The leaders behind the assault were executed without trial. Other members of the conspiracy – Admiral Wilhelm Canaris, the former chief of counter-espionage General Hans Oster, Captain Gehre, Judge Karl Sack, lawyer Hans von Dohnanyi, lawyer and diplomat Adam von Trott zu Solz, and the evangelical priest Dietrich Bonhoeffer – were later brought to court, sentenced to death, and hanged.

The assassination attempt on Hitler was seen as treason, and, not surprisingly, Hitler's popularity soared among the population as a result of it. After the war, the conspirators remained traitors not only in the view of the general population but also according to the law. In 1951, a legal attempt was made to have the sentences annulled, but this was unsuccessful. A Munich court stated that they 'had been sentenced for treason in accordance with prevailing law', i.e. six years after the war, a West German court declared a Nazi summary court to be legal.

It took time for the situation to change in the Federal Republic, but when it did, the change was dramatic. All of a sudden the 'traitors' were transformed into 'heroes' – heroes and symbols of the German resistance, symbols of 'the other Germany'. From then on, this was the new 'truth', and this was what the aspiring nation needed. As von Stauffenberg was useful for this new purpose, it did not really matter that the biggest hero of all, before having swapped side as the war started to go wrong, had served the Führer as a loyal army officer for eleven long years, four of those in a criminal war of aggression. Von Stauffenberg was from now on the good German – and one day even the film star Tom Cruise would give the myth a boost.

Chapter 13

Fold Your Hands for the Führer

On 30 January 1933, Adolf Hitler was declared Chancellor of Germany. With lofty declarations and assurances, lies and deceit, this man had acquired immense power. With propaganda he would hold on to it and further strengthen his power over his people. 'You can be assured that this state will not be broken down in a thousand years from now,' Hitler declared at a party meeting in the state of Thüringen. From now on there would be a constant emphasis on 'us' and 'them' and, not least, on the greatness and potential of the own people and their (to be extended) Fatherland. The building up of a new image was under way, an image of strength and high self-esteem – all aimed at boosting national morale. It was preparation for the war that was to come and it followed the principle 'You deserve it'; or, as propaganda minister Goebbels claimed in *Der Angriff* (The Attack), the magazine he had founded himself: 'It is our destiny to belong to a superior race. A lesser race needs less space, less clothing, less food and culture than a superior one.' Those words were among the first allusions to the expansionist policy to come.

After that day private and official life radically changed in the whole country. Common courtesy became less important and a change in people's behaviour was soon perceptible, all in line with the new teaching. An element of distrust filtered through the population (with the emergence of the Gestapo, there was good reason) and the polite greeting of lifting the hat was spurned in favour of the 'German greeting' – the arm lifted straight forward in what we now know as the Nazi salute. In public offices, in many shops, beer cellars and restaurants, posters exhorted the populace with texts such as 'If you as a German enter this locality, your greeting must be "Heil Hitler"' or 'Town and country greets happily with heart, mouth and hand – Heil Hitler'. Also, any swastika flag carried by marching columns had to be met by the raised arm salute; the loss of reason was total. Nazism permeated the whole country.

It may have been completely distasteful and utterly repulsive – no words can truly convey the antipathy most of us feel when thinking about these happenings – but what lay behind such a change in public mood was a masterly piece of propaganda theory. How this was worded we can discover if we look into Hitler's *Mein Kampf*:

> Propaganda must always address itself to the broad masses of the people [...] All propaganda must be presented in a popular form and must fix its intellectual level so as not to be above the heads of the least intellectual of those to whom it is directed [...]

The art of propaganda consists precisely in being able to awaken the imagination of the public through an appeal to their feelings, in finding the appropriate psychological form that will arrest the attention and appeal to the hearts of the national masses. The broad masses of the people are not made up of diplomats or professors of public jurisprudence nor simply of persons who are able to form reasoned judgment in given cases, but a vacillating crowd of human children who are constantly wavering between one idea and another [...] The great majority of a nation is so feminine in its character and outlook that its thought and conduct are ruled by sentiment rather than by sober reasoning. This sentiment, however, is not complex, but simple and consistent. It is not highly differentiated, but has only the negative and positive notions of love and hatred, right and wrong, truth and falsehood.

As to the methods to be employed, he explains:

Propaganda must not investigate the truth objectively and, in so far as it is favourable to the other side, present it according to the theoretical rules of justice; yet it must present only that aspect of the truth which is favourable to its own side [...] The receptive powers of the masses are very restricted, and their understanding is feeble. On the other hand, they quickly forget. Such being the case, all effective propaganda must be confined to a few bare essentials and those must be expressed as far as possible in stereotyped formulas. These slogans should be persistently repeated until the very last individual has come to grasp the idea that has been put forward [...] Every change that is made in the subject of a propagandist message must always emphasize the same conclusion. The leading slogan must of course be illustrated in many ways and from several angles, but in the end one must always return to the assertion of the same formula.

And so it was; the same assertion was repeated over and over again: 'It is our destiny to belong to a superior race,' – Joseph Goebbels.

It might disturb some, but I have a feeling that even after the demise of the Third Reich these principles have continued to be used in order to build public support for the military campaigns of various states into countries and territories where the aggressor in reality has or had no right to be. Moreover, when it comes to children as targets for 'information', there are similarities between past and present. Here, Adolf Hitler also knew what he was doing: his indoctrination work was not aimed just at the adult population. It started with the smallest of children. In nursery schools the Führer to an extent even replaced God – at least when it came to saying grace:

> Fold your hands
> Bow your head
> Think about the Führer
> Who gives us our daily bread
> And leads us out of every need.

For schools the instructions were:

> Teachers and pupils greet each other with the German greeting. Before each lesson the teacher steps forward in front of the class and greets by lifting the right arm with the words 'Heil Hitler'. The class should respond similarly.

Realising the true extent of this propaganda and what it did, not least to the younger generation, those who fought the war with their own bodies, I can better understand how Peter Schilling was naïve enough to try and preach Nazi propaganda to a group of partisans in a Belgrade bar. How could he have known any better? Whether the older generation, the 'vacillating crowd of human children', should have, I will leave to others to decide.

Chapter 14

Not All Germans are Nazis

Ludwig had decided on his own that the war was not for him, that he did not want to be part of it. Members of the French Resistance movement had helped him and his friend Kurt on their way. Apart from giving practical help to soldiers who wanted to leave, the Resistance also actively encouraged desertion. This was done mainly with the help of illegal newsletters which were secretly spread among the troops. German resistance groups and German civilians also participated in this work. Two of those honourable individuals were Hanns Kralik and his wife Lya.

In 1943, some French friends asked the couple to go to Lyon as co-workers in the 'Committee for a Free Germany'. After the Red Army had won the battles of Stalingrad and Kursk, thus starting the big turnaround in the war, German resistance groups increased their activities in France. The emphasis of their work was now on the German soldiers in the country. Hanns Kralik had for a long time done resistance work with both words and illustrations. His last calling was now the production of illegal papers, leaflets, posters and handbills to display and distribute among German soldiers in the south of France. Such a commission for a professional graphic artist such as Kralik was nothing new, but the financial means to procure paper and other printing materials was unfortunately very limited. Printing facilities were also very difficult to find. As a result of this shortage of resources, an attic printing house was set up in the home of Kralik and his wife in Lyon and here publications like *Freies Deutschland* (A Free Germany), *Unser Vaterland* (Our Fatherland), *Soldat am Mittelmeer* (Soldier at the Mediterranean) and *Der Ausweg* (The Way Out) were printed for distribution. Also leaflets were printed with texts such as 'He who thinks like a German, feels like a German, and he who is faithful to the Fatherland breaks with Hitler and ends the war.'

I heard of this remarkable couple for the first time as I talked to the third main character of this book, Helmut Kober. Starting his story, Helmut said:

It was in 1953 or maybe the year after. The phone rang and a man presented himself as Hanns Kralik. 'Are you Helmut Kober?' he said. I affirmed and he continued, 'I have read articles by you in the newspaper. You are my comrade. Please come and visit us. My wife and I would so much like to meet you and talk.' Such an invitation I was very happy to accept. Hanns Kralik was a draftsman and designer, a well-known artist. I went to the river front of Düsseldorf, to the old town where the couple lived, and was received as a most welcome guest. We seated ourselves at a table in front of a big window with a view over the Rhine. Mrs Kralik served coffee and cakes and her husband offered a real French cognac. 'A souvenir from our French friends,' he said softly. After that lovely opening, an afternoon spent exchanging memories from the war started.

Helmut Kober was born in Gladbeck, a mining town in the Ruhr district not far from Düsseldorf. Helmut's father was a social democrat and member of the *Deutsche Freidenker-Verband* (German Association of Freethinkers) – an organisation based on a secular and scientific view of life. The young Helmut himself was a member of *Die Falken* (The Falcons), the social democratic organisation for children under the age of fourteen. Later in life he continued to follow in his father's footsteps, becoming a lifelong freethinking author in his own right.

In 1933, as Hitler came to power, Helmut was still only a young boy. Nonetheless, he already saw for himself the first signs of what was to come. Being a book lover, the young lad was horrified as the new rulers started to burn publications they did not like. Hearing at first-hand how Goebbels denounced great authors' books as 'dirt and rubbish' literature was an experience the young boy would never forget. With his own early love of great literature and art, it was impossible for Helmut fully to comprehend what the propaganda minister was screaming about. After all, what Goebbels called 'dirt' were works by famous German writers – writers loved by the whole nation. No, he could not believe what he was witnessing. Unbelievable, but nevertheless true: German professors in SS uniforms and students in Hitler Youth uniforms were actually throwing thousands and thousands of valuable books onto bonfires.

This kind of behaviour could never be allowed to become a part of Helmut's world, and he would stand his ground. 'I distanced myself from all Nazi organisations and from an early age I experienced many difficulties, but I did not give in.' From these early days it was clear to Helmut what was going on. 'And,' as he said years later, 'of course the general public knew about the arrests and deportations.' Yes, of course, they had heard of the camps, and how could they not have noticed the boycott of Jewish shops? After all, they took part in it themselves. At the very least, anybody could have seen the effect that the Nuremberg race laws had on the community. How could anybody claim not to know? After all, much of it was written into the legislation, and it happened over the whole country – in broad daylight.

Looking back, Helmut never really understood those people who – in the years after the war – claimed ignorance and political disinterest as a defence against co-responsibility. He continued:

There had been constant reminders of the ongoing evil all the way up to the start of the war. If not before, at least the Crystal Night of 9-10 November 1938 should have been the final wake-up call, but for most people it wasn't.

If they had seen the hordes of Nazis and SS troops storm through the towns and cities, plundering synagogues, demolishing houses, killing and maiming (and all people had), what more was there to be in doubt about?

It was all organised, and on this gruesome night it was directed at the Jewish part of the population. They were pulled out on the streets and beaten up; they were forced to walk with bare feet across broken glass, but [as Helmut reminds us all these years later] even in a long-established newspaper like the *Gladbecker Zeitung* these thuggish riots were referred to the day after as 'a spontaneous action of the people'.

When this happened, Helmut was sixteen and living with his family at Hindenburgstrasse. Across the road from them was a Jewish family. They were all beaten up and their home and shop were demolished. Further down the road there was another Jewish shopkeeper, a shoemaker, and his business was also totally demolished by the Nazi mob. During that night a total of 26,000 Jewish citizens were arrested and sent to concentration camps. On top of that, ninety-one people were killed and 265 synagogues destroyed.

One might think that such huge nationwide destruction, mainly of Jewish life and property, would have given rise to serious reflection – and disgust. But it did not. By and large, people were enthusiastic, and it was said that 'it had been a great success for the party'. Though it had not been the general population that had been behind the devastation, it is important to remember that people had seen what had happened and, even worse, rather than try to defend those attacked, many 'ordinary citizens' had joined the SA gangs and helped out. As is so often the case with human beings and difficult moral issues, between those who actively killed and destroyed and those few who went to great efforts to protect their endangered fellow citizens a great majority of passive individuals just stayed out of it, subsequently chose the winning side and adapted to the new political reality.

Unfortunately, this night of destruction was only a taste of what was to come. A year later Poland would be attacked and this would lead to an unwilling military career for a young person who, if he could have made the choice himself, would rather have spent his time with art and literature.

In 1940, Helmut was drafted into the *Luftgau-Nachrichten-Regiment 2* in Posen, a unit responsible for the use of teleprinters and telephone connections. Here he acquired three driving licences, was trained as a telegraph operator, and during most of the war served in the Signal Corps behind the front. In this position Helmut bore witness to immense suffering of people in other countries, all caused by the German occupation. He became familiar with the ghettos of Warsaw, Vilnius and Minsk, he saw what was going on there, and he saw what was happening in other areas where the *Wehrmacht* and the Nazi administration had taken over.

Helmut witnessed the evil with his own eyes. But on the radio he also listened to the news, the same information that everyone else in the country had access to. There could be no doubt as to the intent of the Nazis.

How could you keep believing this was a war of defence after hearing your own leader screaming on the radio: 'Thousands of German fighter planes will attack London. The big proud city will become all fire! I will eradicate their cities.' After all, this was what Hitler cried out in his radio speeches to his ever growing numbers of ecstatic followers.

Helmut Kober.

Brandenburg, 9 October 1940

Dear parents, dear sisters,

This will be my last letter home. On 14 September I was sentenced to death by the Reich War Court. This evening I have been told that the sentence will be executed early tomorrow morning. Therefore, in this letter I would like to thank you all from the bottom of my heart for all the love and care you have always shown me, and I will ask you all to forgive me for all the pain and suffering I have brought upon you. Lately I have prayed a lot for you, as I have been in solitary confinement for some weeks. I thought at least in that way I could be of some help, if ever so little. When you read this letter I shall no longer be alive. I am calm and in peace, as I have had time to prepare myself for what is to come.

Your Josef

However, it was not just ordinary people who joined in the enthusiasm following the initial success in combat and conquest. Even the Evangelical Church showed great interest in the development, and it did not seem that they were against what was taking place. For example, before the war 598,900 out of the 835,200 Evangelical Christians in Poland were of German descent. Now they would be back in the German fold. This caused a flood of congratulations and welcoming words to be sent from congregations within the 'motherland'. Some of these letters have been made public. The *Evangelische Reichsfrauenhilfe* (Evangelical Reich Women's Aid) wrote to its sister organisation in Danzig: 'After twenty years of hardship and after months of hard struggle you have been liberated thanks to the Führer's action [...] We greet you with the strongest comforting words of our God.' Another welcoming message, written to the 'liberated' Evangelical sisters and brothers in Reichsgau Wartheland stated that a 'wonder had happened'. It went on, 'Your hopes have been fulfilled. God has heard your prayer. He has sent the Führer to liberate you from twenty years of forced Polish dominance.'

As Helmut expressed it, 'At the same time as Warsaw was being bombarded and Catholics murdered, German bishops prayed to their God that he should protect the Third Reich and its *Wehrmacht.*'

Mr and Mrs Wegener

Helmut was heavily influenced by a family with very strong ethical convictions. His uncle Erich who lived nearby, was an example of that. Erich had been declared 'a first class state enemy' and, as a direct consequence, had been sacked without notice from his job at the state railway. What in the end had caused his uncle's dismissal was that he and his wife had been very supportive of another couple in the neighbourhood, a couple in which the wife was Jewish.

For Mr and Mrs Wegener times were extremely difficult. As was the case with all other Jews' rationing cards, a big 'J' had been stamped on hers. This 'J' prevented her from buying various essential victuals, banned her from the local library, excluded her from public transport and even hindered her from going to the hairdresser. In fact, it prevented her from doing almost anything, and she was allowed nothing. She had even been ordered to deliver all her valuable things, including some clothes, to the authorities, without compensation of course. In fact, as it was for all other Jews at the time, she had been deprived of all rights.

Uncle Erich told Helmut about this when his nephew came home on leave. 'So what do people do about it?' the young man asked. His uncle replied:

> There have been a lot of changes. There are people here who, before times changed, showed compassion and solidarity with their fellow citizens. Today you cannot be so sure about many of them. Most of them look the other way when 'things happen'. They don't want to know; they don't want to see or hear. 'It's only about Jews,' they seem to think.

Mr and Mrs Wegener were not even allowed to share the air raid shelter with their neighbours when the sirens sounded; they had to sit in the stairwell. And, on the streets, nobody greeted them any longer; people looked the other way. The husband, an actor, had *Berufsverbot* (prohibition) and was not allowed to work in his profession, as he was married to a Jew. As Helmut's uncle said: 'Twelve thousand Jewish soldiers died for the Kaiser on the battlefields of the First World War, and this is how they say "thank you".'

Having somebody to talk to, somebody he knew would not turn him in, was good for Helmut's uncle. One recent event especially was constantly on his mind, and it was a very painful one – he could not stop thinking about it. It had happened only days before he got the sack. A freight train had arrived and had been parked at the shunting area awaiting final departure for Auschwitz. There were several wagons, all of them crammed with people – men, women and children. They were unable to sit or lie down, packed closely together. For hours the wagons were standing there waiting for the order to move, and one could see the poor souls' eyes as they looked through the cracks of the otherwise sealed wagons. One could hear quiet moaning and crying. 'Of course,' Erich said, shortly before the Wegeners were due to come for an evening meal, 'of course they all know. It's genocide we talk about, and they, the people, they all know.'

Helmut was shocked, though hardly surprised. After all, he himself had seen how Jews were treated in the occupied areas where he was forced to serve. On a daily basis he had witnessed the humiliation and brutality they were exposed to. They were not even allowed to walk on the footpaths outside the ghettos; they had to walk on the street, and he had often seen cars and horse carts deliberately try to drive into them. If these people then approached a German soldier, like himself, they had take off their cap or hat; women had to greet the German so that it could clearly be heard.

Cilli Josephs, Bremen

Helmut recalled:

> On a building site near Minsk, a group of Jews from the ghetto worked for several weeks. I collected them every morning in a lorry and drove them back again in the evening. A Jewish sports student from Vienna belonged to this group of forced labourers. He trusted me and we often talked together. A staff sergeant, with whom I could talk openly, frequently gave me bread, sausages, butter and other provisions that I passed on to the young student, who in turn distributed them to others.

One day at the beginning of May 1943, the young student asked Helmut to talk to him in private. He was distraught and in a very low mood. During one work break the two men sat down and Helmut tried to cheer him up. But then the young man said with a trembling voice: 'Tomorrow we will not come to work. They will take us away and shoot us. Do not tell any of the others; they don't know anything yet.' Helmut tried to distract him and comfort him, but he would not countenance it:

> No, don't try that, we are not the first to be killed. Thank you for being so kind to us. It has been a blessing for all of us. With your friendly words and many good deeds you have made our fate much easier. All the time we have felt your compassion. We hope that you will survive this evil time.

Helmut continued:

As a memory he gave me a book by Henrik Ibsen, and I have kept it carefully with me ever since. In the book is handwritten 'Cilli Josephs, Bremen'. Maybe Cilli Josephs had given it to the young Jew before she herself was shot.

The next day, Helmut saw long columns of Jews being taken away. The site of the crime was a few kilometres from the town and the victims were made to walk or were driven by lorries. There, they were all shot. The main perpetrators were from the SS and SD (the Nazi Security Service, a police organisation tasked with secret intelligence missions) but members of the regular armed forces took part as well.

At one point, Helmut drove almost daily into Minsk in order to take people to day jobs outside of the ghetto. It horrified him to see the suffering there; it was the most horrible place. Weak and enfeebled men were everywhere; women and children were lying and sitting on the streets. The daily ration of food, he was later told, was a thin watery soup with a few grams of buckwheat and, added to that, 150 grams of bread. He also found out that by the end of 1941, already around 30,000 people had died from illnesses and starvation in this place.

The border of the ghetto was guarded by SS troops, but within it was policed by a Jewish guard service, the *Ordnungsdienst*. Sometimes Helmut talked to these guards about different matters. One of those short conversations he especially remembered very clearly years after. He had just arrived to collect his workers, when one of these members of the *Ordnungsdienst* – a former German officer who in the First World War had been awarded the Iron Cross – pointed out another van right beside them. 'That is no delivery van,' he said; 'at least not one of the usual sort.' The van Helmut was facing was, as he now learned, a special vehicle for killing people. It was a *Gaswagen*, a 'gas van' – a mobile gas chamber.

'I cannot believe it,' Helmut said. 'First we didn't either,' the decorated Jewish war veteran, himself a potential future victim of this death van, replied. He could tell more: seventy to eighty people at a time could be transported this way. At the end of the road, the now dead 'cargo' would be delivered to a mass grave. Human inventiveness had reached a new low.

These exterminator machines were originally Himmler's idea. He wanted to diminish the psychological stress caused to the killers, especially when exterminating children. However, as with all new inventions, this one had its problems. As the act of killing – murdering the 'passengers' by transferring the van's exhaust gas into a sealed chamber – was a slow process, the screams from the terrified victims would cause considerable distress to the driver. So the executioners' working conditions had not been improved much and the use of the vans remained marginal. Later information has revealed that the van that Helmut saw was one of three which were in use in and around Minsk. According to the death squad's own numbers, these vans killed close to 100,000 people. Though this number is frightening, it still only makes up a small part of all those who were murdered.

Helmut paused to reflect:

All the dreadful crimes I witnessed, which were committed by the German occupying forces in the Soviet Union, Lithuania, Poland and other countries, angered me tremendously and have been a terrible burden to my conscience ever since. After all, I was German, and I wore the uniform with the Nazi bird. I have seen in Minsk how the SS, the armed forces and the police hunted hundreds of Jewish men, women and children through the streets and how they drove them on lorries to extermination sites outside the town. It was at such moments that I was ashamed of my nationality.

Above international law

What Helmut Kober had experienced while on *Wehrmacht* duty in Minsk and elsewhere was in fact nothing but the fulfilment of what had been proclaimed at the outset of the invasion of the Soviet Union, the Russian Campaign. In March 1941, a few months before the start of the attack, Hitler demanded of the high military command a guarantee that the invasion would be merciless. 'A war against the Soviet Union cannot be carried out in a gentlemanly way,' he asserted. The stage was set for a showdown between two ideologies, and this campaign should therefore, as it was said, be carried out with unprecedented brutality; no compassion should be shown. In line with that general instruction, it was commanded, for example, that escaping prisoners of war should be shot immediately without warning and that executions of Communists should be enacted in a way that in itself would have a further deterrent effect. The same lack of mercy would be shown to their own soldiers: if anybody did not use his weapon when ordered to do so, or, alternatively, did not use it lustily enough, he would make himself liable to punishment.

The ambition was no longer only military conquest but the total extinction of all the rights of the regime's opponents to exist as free people. German colonisation would reach all the way to the Urals, and in all annexed territories the alleged racially inferior indigenous people would be enslaved. *Generalplan Ost* (General Plan for the East) was the official name of the planned Germanising and colonisation of the east European countries. As part of these extensive plans, the Soviet state was to be destroyed, part of the local population would be exterminated and some of the others, the luckier ones, would be transferred to Siberia. Those Russians who would be allowed to stay would be used as forced labour for the new masters.

'I served in the Brandenburg division. In the Kiev area it was found out one day that supplies had been stolen from our food storage. Russian civilians in the area were starving [and they were blamed]. The whole unit was commanded in action. The entire nearby village was ordered to be destroyed, levelled to the ground. That was the moment when I finally had had enough. All these people were to be slaughtered, all of them. I saw mothers with their children in their arms and I said to myself: No, I won't do that. But then I was in serious trouble myself; it would

be refusal to obey orders. Sorry, but no, no, I couldn't do such a thing; I shot
along the ground. It was noticed, and I was pulled out …'

Lothar Pfeiffer

In Helmut's unit in Minsk in 1942, one could sign up for future assignments after
the takeover of farms in eastern Russia. One could, for example, be a supervisor and
oversee the work of these future Russian slaves. Goebbels' propaganda had completely
changed people's minds. What before would have been seen as criminal was now legal;
what would have been seen as profoundly wrong, perfectly right. This new mentality
had completely taken over, and there was nothing left to prevent it from getting even
worse. As Hitler said, 'German soldiers who contravene international humanitarian
law can be forgiven.'

Call for cease-fire

On 8 January 1943, Gen. Konstantin Rokossovsky, whose troops had helped encircle
the German Sixth Army at Stalingrad, called for a cease-fire and offered his opponent,
Field Marshal Friedrich Paulus, very generous terms if he would surrender and stop the
slaughter. But Paulus was in a difficult position. His army was dressed poorly for the
extreme cold; the numbers of dead and wounded were enormous, and the supply lines
were strained to the limit; in fact, they were more or less cut. Still, Paulus would not
surrender. Though being the commander-in-chief of the whole operation, he was not
authorised to make such a decision himself. Paulus had to ask the Führer for permission,
and that request, as expected, was refused straight away. Hitler, safe in Berlin, at least
for the time being, ordered Paulus and his troops to stay put and fight until there was
nobody left standing. Faced with this, the slaughter continued. But the situation was
desperate. As Paulus informed the Chancellor that only hours were left before the final
catastrophe, Hitler's response was to advise him to commit suicide. If not, he was told,
he would shame Germany's military history.

Whether or not Paulus in the end shamed Germany's name, others will decide.
But, as a turncoat, it could be argued that he shamed his own. On 31 January, he and
his closest staff surrendered, and two days later the last sections of the army did the
same. If Hitler was raging about that shameful end to the fighting, he would rage even
more when a few months later he heard about the Field Marshal's new commitment.
Now, being a prisoner of war, Paulus had decided to join the resistance, the German
opposition in exile.

Encouraged by the political branch of the Red Army, the National Committee for a
Free Germany (NKFD) was founded in a small town close to Moscow on 12 July 1943.
The exiled German Communist writer Erich Weinert became its president, and two
former *Wehrmacht* officers, now prisoners of war, were appointed as his deputies. The

leadership of the organisation was to have thirty-eight members, and of those ten were Communists who had been exiled from Germany before the war, among them Walter Ulbricht and Wilhelm Pieck. The remaining twenty-eight were prisoners of war. The aim of the NKFD was not only to 'inform and guide' other German prisoners of war in Russia but also to reach out to soldiers still serving on the enemy side. Useful for this purpose were newsletters and leaflets that could be scattered from aircraft over enemy lines. But also loudspeakers at the front and radio transmissions would be used to get the message across. The aim was to get soldiers to change side, to desert.

This was the context in which Field Marshal Paulus found himself as a co-worker. Paulus had been commander of an army that had lost three quarters of a million men in one single battle. Now, after he had been forced to surrender, he was asking those still alive to desert from their units – well knowing what would happen to them if they were caught. It might be argued that this man would have had a better chance to go down in history as a peacemaker had he swapped sides long before all these men and their Russian counterparts had been sacrificed on the battlefield. He did not do that, but he did it in time to save his own skin, and he was lucky. Paulus had been commander-in-chief of an army that had waged a genocidal war against the Communist Soviet Union; he had used his remarkable military skills in support of the Nazis, but, even so, after the war he was allowed to retire to *Communist* East Germany as a respectable citizen. However, that last achievement was not as unusual as it might sound; Paulus was far from being the only top Nazi figure who got away with it. There were many, and we will return to that later.

Chapter 15

Secret Meeting in Paris

Helmut Kober had heard of the National Committee for a Free Germany. For him it was increasingly clear that desertion was his only remaining option; he had to join the resistance. He could stay no longer; he could no longer be part of a criminal war. Helmut started to plan a way out. However, before he could carry out his plans he would see himself in a completely different situation – the unit he belonged to was transferred to France.

It was in the spring of 1944 that Helmut arrived in a suburb of Paris. He had not managed to defect in the east, but, soon and by pure chance, another opportunity to join the resistance would present itself. Helmut had applied for leave in order to seek dental treatment at a military hospital in a more central part of the capital. He left for the city on the Métro and got off at Gare Saint-Lazare. Shortly thereafter a man approached him in the street.

'Sorry, comrade, have you got a light?'

Helmut found his lighter, lit the man's cigarette and asked curiously: 'A German in civilian clothes? Are you employed in the public service?'

'Can we walk a few steps?' the stranger asked. They started to move, and he continued: 'I'm an Austrian from Vienna and have lived here in Paris for a while. I'm not in the army or in any public service. Are you stationed here in Paris?'

'Only since very recently,' Helmut replied. 'I'm in the Signal Corps. I don't know Paris very well.'

'Are you a Nazi?' the Austrian asked. Helmut was taken by surprise by the brash question; he thought for a moment and decided to take a major risk.

'I am not a Nazi; I never was and I will never be one.'

The Austrian gave him his hand. 'You are a comrade. My name is Ernst, and as an anti-Fascist I had to flee Vienna; I now live as an immigrant in Paris. I belong to the French resistance group *Résistance*. So what about you? What are you doing?'

Helmut, delighted to have found someone who shared his views, answered that he came from a social democratic home and that his father and uncle had both been sacked from their jobs by the authorities and were being persecuted. He had supported the resistance himself back home and as a soldier in the east.

'I'm more than ready to help if I can,' Helmut said.

Ernst smiled happily. 'Then I don't need to lecture you about our responsibility towards the people here and the German people. You realise that resistance is primarily about breaking the Fascist terror and that we all must help erase the awful blemish that these criminals have smeared the German people with. You shall seek two reliable comrades and then start a group,' Ernst said. 'You and I will meet on a regular basis and each meeting will be in a different location, a mutually agreed place. From now on I am your liaison person and need information from you regarding your unit's plans and movements of troops. I also need to know the mood among your comrades and the officers. If possible, don't write anything down. Memorise all details and tell me next time I see you. I'm a good listener and have an excellent memory.'

Helmut was told he should work not only within his unit but anywhere he met soldiers. For the task he would receive leaflets and miniature posters. This material would be well hidden in cream cans, biscuit boxes and cigarette packs, and as an example Ernst gave him a cigarette box in which there were two A5-size posters. Both of these had a graphic with a text. The first showed a soldier hanging on some barbed wire, and underneath was written:

Total war
Death at the front and at home
Save yourselves and your family
Fight for peace.

On the next poster soldiers were pictured carrying a banner with the text:

March back to Germany
Overthrow Hitler
Save people and homeland.

After this first coincidental meeting, Ernst and Helmut met secretly at different places along the Seine about twice a week for the next three months. In between those encounters Helmut, helped by two trustworthy friends, distributed leaflets to parked army vehicles and to the soldiers' toilets. They also left them in cinemas frequented by soldiers and at the air force café at Rue de l'Élysée. The message was:

Stop the fighting, let France be free!
Don't shoot at Frenchmen.
Don't participate in arrests, shooting of hostages or informing.
Hitler's removal will save Germany and lead to peace.
If you are sent to the east, defect to the Red Army who also fight
in the coalition against Hitler

As Helmut's unit was moved again, three months later, the co-operation with Ernst came to an abrupt end. But for a young man who wanted to fight for what was right, it had been an extremely important time.

'On the Roof of the World there is a Stork's Nest'

After D-Day, the Allied invasion of Normandy on 6 June 1944, Helmut's unit was again on the move – this time in retreat. As the end of the war came closer, Helmut was back in the east, now as part of the infamous Gen. Schörner's troops, fighting the advancing Red Army in Upper Silesia. He could hardly have been worse off. Of all the brutal officers commanding troops during the Second World War, Ferdinand Schörner is the one with the worst reputation. There are numerous reports of this man's extreme brutality against his own soldiers. The tiniest wrong-doing would be severely punished. As he boasted, he preferred them to be hanged instead of shot: 'We shall let them hang in front of the soldiers' holiday homes and at railway stations. Three days the bodies must hang – until they stink. That's good for morale.'

We know that this is what happened to soldiers under Schörner's command, but that these comments were documented was due to an SS lawyer, Freiherr von Dörnberg. 'Please notice, Herr Judge,' Schörner said to him one day, 'my judges have to learn to do wrong.' Von Dörnberg found the comments extraordinary, as he knew that only shooting was allowed as a method of killing. Allowed or not, after the *Wehrmacht* had capitulated, Schörner's men were found everywhere, hanging from trees and lamp posts. Helmut could easily have ended up the same way, but I am happy to say that was not his destiny.

> At night we had to lay out barbed wire and landmines in no man's land between the combating troops. Suddenly random shooting started and our little group had to seek cover. Then suddenly silence fell and we could hear the hit song *'Auf dem Dach der Welt da steht ein Storchennest'* ['On the Roof of the World there is a Stork's Nest']

Allied forces find a traitor hanging from a tree.

being played. It was awesome and eerie in the nightly silence over a battlefield. Then the music stopped and we heard a voice clearly say that he was speaking to us for the National Committee for a Free Germany.

The voice on the speakers ended with the words: 'A break in shooting for a few minutes will follow. Use the chance to defect to the other side. We have food for you and soon you can go home.' However, nobody crossed over. A German officer ordered 'Fire!' and the German troops shot extensively at where the speakers were thought to be. That was the point when Helmut and his soldier friends decided to run over to the Russians. 'Helmut, you take command,' one man said. 'You're a corporal; it's even a grade higher than the Führer!' Helmut agreed, and at an opportune moment during the night they reported to a guard in a Russian trench.

In the PoW camp we were taken to afterwards, we were introduced to the National Committee and its members. Their password 'Fight Hitler, put an end to the war, punish the criminals of war and rebuild a free and democratic Germany' resonated with me and I declared myself a co-worker. As a broadcaster at the Ukrainian front shortly after, I delivered my first radio speech, encouraging my friends to defect. In my ten-minute speech I said: 'I know only too well that many of you are under the influence of propaganda against the Soviet Union and others. This propaganda says better dead than in captivity and it is better that I spare a bullet for an honourable death. Comrades, don't do it! It would be a death shrouded in dishonour. The homeland needs you. Our Fatherland needs good patriotic Germans. The traitors sit comfortably in their reinforced bunkers and preach about endurance at the front and at home. They play with the lives of German soldiers and they harass our women and children. Help us free Germany from this Fascist terror and defect from all parts of the front. The war is lost! Stop fighting and turn your weapons on Hitler and those who try to force you to take a catastrophic course. Defecting is about Germany's fate and your families' lives. Germany needs the living, and enough have died. I beseech all of you not to follow Hitler and his henchmen. I beg you to oppose prolonging of the war. The purpose of such pleading is to end the war for the benefit and salvation of our people.'

Gen. Ferdinand Schörner, who had been promoted by Hitler to commander-in-chief of the army on 30 April 1945, deserted to Austria a week later, in order to avoid being taken prisoner by the Soviets. Twelve years later, in October 1957, the general was charged with one case of manslaughter and two cases of attempted murder committed during the war. He was found guilty and sentenced to four and a half years in prison. The prosecutor had asked for eight years, but the West German court took the general's military achievements and personal bravery into account as mitigating circumstances. After having served two years of his sentence, Schörner was released from prison.

Later Helmut was told that this speech had been heard by his unit and that, in absentia, he had been sentenced to death for desertion, instigating desertion and assisting the enemy. However, the military judges and their executioners would never get their hands on Helmut. Shortly after, in Ostrava in Moravia, in what today is part of the Czech Republic, he saw the end of the war. Thereafter he spent time in a succession of camps – in Pardubice, Auschwitz and Tiflis (now Tbilisi), Georgia – before being allowed to return home in 1948:

> I suffered indescribably from the dreadful experiences during the war, witnessing the criminal acts committed by my fellow Germans in the Soviet Union and other occupied countries. It had long been a burden on my conscience and desertion therefore gave me a chance to ease this burden just a little. It made it somewhat easier for me to live with the deep shame and immense anger that filled me in those days and that still fills me today when I think about the heinous crimes committed against my fellow Europeans and the genocide of the Jews and others. That step has calmed my soul somewhat, and I am glad I had the courage to resist and to desert, even if my friends and I are still jeered at as traitors by self-declared pseudo patriots.

> Work for peace among people
> And between nations
> Keep and take care of this world
> It belongs to our children.

Helmut Kober, 2001

Chapter 16

The Refugee Returns

After three months in Witzwil, Peter Schilling was transferred to a new camp in Aarau in the Swiss canton of Aargau. Here he met Alfred, a young Communist, for whom everything was either black or white, good or bad, noble or ignoble. For this young man there was nothing in between, no nuances, but for Peter he was a light in a dark, murderous world:

> Alfred was a good and reliable friend, and, of course, I wanted to be like him. I was completely taken aback by his enthusiasm and wanted to walk the same true path as him, or so I thought – the path to a peaceful and equal future.

The enthusiastic young man further helped shape Peter's view of the world, but their time together was to be short and they were soon to go their separate ways. Alfred disappeared, most likely, as he had said, in order to join the Communist resistance, and Peter was transferred to a working camp in Murimoos. However, by this point he had made his final decision. He would do as Alfred had done; he also would leave and join the resistance. In July 1944, Peter absconded from the camp with the plan to join the French partisans.

Having lost contact with Alfred, Peter found another friend who would join him in his new venture. Claes was a young Dutchman who had voluntarily joined the Luftwaffe after having been convinced by Goebbels' propaganda that this was the right way. But, as with Peter, it had not taken long for Claes to figure out the truth behind the speeches. Having done that, he decided he would no longer howl with the Nazi wolves.

From other prisoners at the camp the two prospective freedom fighters had got necessary information and addresses of people in France who would issue them with false IDs. It would be a dangerous undertaking, but neither man doubted that they had to go back and join the Hitler opposition. Therefore, in the midst of a thunderstorm, they crossed the border to France, back into Nazi controlled territory. Unfortunately, though their route had been well planned, Claes and Peter soon lost their bearings. They had no idea where they were, and it was not easy to ask for help; it was dangerous for local people to support refugees, there was a constant risk of being denounced, and in some places there was no point even trying. For example, it was best to stay away from wealthy-looking farms. If a door was ever opened, it was immediately shut again.

However, as usual, there are people out there who, in spite of the danger to themselves, happily protect those in need. It was late afternoon/early evening as the two young men, totally exhausted and with empty stomachs, came to a peaceful village at the edge of the forest. At first they hesitated; they wanted to make up their minds carefully before getting any closer. Danger? They saw a church and thought the house beside it must be the vicarage. Finally they went over, knocked on the door, but got no reaction. As they left, they were spotted by a young girl standing with a pram in front of a poor-looking peasant cottage. She was trying to calm a wailing baby. As the men passed her, she spoke: 'You wanted to see the vicar; he will be back in about two hours. You must be hungry, come with me.'

Hesitating, Peter and Claes entered the impoverished dwelling. Inside was the father, who looked at the newcomers and wanted to know where they had come from and where they were heading. The young men replied in an evasive way, and the man continued: 'These days so many are on their way, and they are all hungry. Please, take a seat at the table.' The little girl had left while they were talking, and now she returned with a piece of bread. She was followed by some neighbours who all added to the table – a few eggs from one, a piece of cheese from another, and a bit of sausage from a third. It was a display of overwhelming kindness in such a difficult time. However, the refugees felt uneasy – after all, now so many knew about them. As they were asked to stay overnight, they had to apologise and turn down the kind offer. They feared it might have been too risky. The villagers tried their best to get them to stay, but they understood.

On 6 June 1944, Peter and Claes were finally close to Besançon, their first destination. Then what they had carefully tried to avoid ever since crossing the border happened. Two cycling *gendarmes* approached them on the road. Initially they were not worried; they had met French police before on their way, and none of them seemed to show any interest in finding out who they were. But it was different this time. As the two constables were about to pass, suddenly they jumped off their bikes, drew their guns and arrested the refugees. Now another ordeal began. Peter and Claes were taken to the police headquarters, interviewed and very soon thereafter handed over to the Germans. Their next destination was a local citadel and solitary confinement.

Claes and Peter's common path ended there, and from then on Peter's world, apart from being regularly interviewed and beaten up, was reduced to four steps in one direction and two in the other – all this in a tiny cell equipped with the usual folded-up (only for night use) iron bed, a small wooden table and a stool. A tiny bit of blue sky was visible through a small window close to the ceiling; everything else was dirty grey.

One thing Peter remembered clearly from the first days in this citadel was that he was told by the SD people that in absentia he had been sentenced to death for desertion and *Wehrkraftzersetzung*. Having heard that, there was nothing else to do other than wait for the execution to be carried out. 'Every morning I was waiting for them. I had made up my mind. I would refuse to be blindfolded. I had thought it all through carefully.'

Peter waited. One morning after another he was ready for them to come for him. But nobody came. As he recalled, 'It was difficult to continue being prepared to die. The will to live started to come back. I cried and wailed, and life continued as before: four steps in one direction and two in the other.'

Then one day they did come for Peter. However, not to be shot, but to be taken to Berlin. As expected, in Berlin a military judge awaited him. This judge, however, extremely unusually for the time, showed mercy – probably due to extraordinary circumstances in the build-up to the trial. Peter's father had found a lawyer to defend his son. Barrister Leppin was the brother of a colleague of Revd Schilling. That this lawyer, who had been a long-standing member of the Nazi party and had been richly decorated for his allegiance, would agree to defend a deserter was certainly something quite exceptional and can only be explained by these personal connections. Nevertheless, for Peter this would mean life instead of imminent death.

The defence lawyer's strategy was that the defendant had lost his beloved mother only shortly before he deserted. During his Swiss encampment, he had started to realise what a disgraceful crime he had committed and had decided to return and repay what he owed his country. If he had not been arrested, he would have volunteered to the armed forces under a false identity – in order to help the 'just cause'. Leppin said:

> Even I didn't believe him when I first heard his story. However, as he keeps firmly to this version, though I strongly have stressed he must speak the truth, I have come to the conclusion that there is no reason not to believe that Private Schilling speaks the truth. It is my hope the court will share my view.

And they did. The military court accepted the mitigating aspects in the case, as put forward by the defence lawyer, and instead of upholding the in absentia death sentence, Peter was sentenced to three years' imprisonment for having left his unit without permission – as usual to be served after the war had finished.

However, the case did not end there. The prosecution was not happy with the outcome. Peter was tried again, and this time treason was added to the accusations. Though that charge was not upheld, the final sentence was something like twelve years. The precise number of years Peter could not remember after the war. At the time of the sentencing, it was more or less irrelevant, as he would first have had to serve the time after a Nazi German war victory. Had it ever come to that, it would most likely have made no difference for a person like him on what side of the prison wall he might have found himself.

After this final sentence the returnee deserter was transferred to new destinations, first Torgau and thereafter a penal battalion in Haut-Rhin (Oberelsass) right behind the front. On arriving there, he was told by the commander that in his unit there was no need to expect or hope for any long-term survival.

The regime was brutal and the food was minimal. Evil events happened all the time, but one episode especially would stay with him for the rest of his life. In the camp there was a marked line that it was forbidden to step over. One day a leaflet from an Allied propaganda grenade landed on the other side. When an officer ordered one of the men to pick it up, the prisoner/soldier was unsure what to do; he knew he was not allowed to step over the line, and he knew that if he refused to obey the order, he would be shot on the spot. He stepped over the line, and the same officer shot him in the back – now for attempting to escape.

Peter stayed in this unit only for a short while. During an enemy air attack, he managed to escape once again, despite the fact that he had been badly injured by a grenade splinter. Thereafter the situation in the crumbling Third Reich was completely chaotic, and Peter managed to hide under different identities in hospitals and other military units until it was all over. He saw the end of the war in what is today the Czech Republic. But his feelings were mixed. True, the slaughter had stopped, but he was now a horrified witness to the result of Field Marshal Schörner's terror. 'Traitors' and other military 'criminals' hung from lamp posts and trees along the roads. Schörner's summary courts had been very busy during the last days of the war, and the Field Marshal had managed without them as well. But neither he nor his judges ever had to pay the price for these murders. We will come back to that.

Chapter 17

Smeared and Vilified

As was the case with Peter Schilling, Ludwig Baumann also miraculously survived a stay in a penal battalion and saw the end of the war in the present-day Czech Republic. After having recovered from diphtheria and regained his ability to walk, he had been transferred from Fort Zinna in Torgau to the Eastern Front and *Bewährungsbataillon 500*. For most of his fellow victims this would have been equivalent to a new death sentence; the survival rate in such a battalion was close to nil. For Kurt Oldenburg, who deserted with Ludwig back in Bordeaux, life also ended in one of those battalions.

However, like Peter Schilling, Ludwig survived. He was wounded in Ukraine and treated in a hospital in Bruenn (today Brno), and that sequence of events would finally save his life. The one person who at the end made the difference was a conscripted Czech doctor. This man did his best to delay the healing of the wounds, so that Ludwig's stay in hospital would last as long as possible, ideally to the end of war. For the doctor, this was of course an extremely dangerous thing to do. Had he been found out, he would most likely have been shot immediately, but he was not, so by delaying the cure this brave man saved the young Ludwig's life.

Of course, it was impossible for one man to save them all. In the ward there was another young man who had also been admitted from a penal battalion. As this patient had recovered enough to be sent back to the front, he poured a saucepan of boiling water over himself – all to avoid his fate. He was severely burned. Ludwig does not know what happened to him thereafter, but there is every reason to expect the worse.

By Christmas 1945, Ludwig was back home, but he could not cope with life. His experiences had been far too traumatic to be forgotten from one day to another. And things were not as he had expected them to be; support for a person like him was close to non-existent. Hitler and his cohorts had treated him as a traitor, and in post-war Germany he would continue to be treated as such. This was how it was for them all, those few deserters who had survived. Instead of being legally rehabilitated, having their sentences annulled (the least one might expect) and damages paid for what their persecutors had put them through, the deserters were met with widespread discrimination. For most of them, this discrimination lasted for the rest of their lives, whether in a private or official capacity. This applied even to people from whom we would have reason to expect better.

In post-war West Germany, two organisations aimed at supporting people who had been persecuted by the Nazis were founded. These were the *Verband der Verfolgten des*

Naziregimes (Association for People Persecuted by the Nazi Regime) and the *Verband der Opfer des Faschismus* (Association for the Victims of Fascism). However, not even those organisations wanted to have anything to do with the deserters.

Ludwig was happy to have survived and be back home again, but, as he says today:

> It was like this: the few of us who had survived the war were not only physically in tatters but also totally destroyed in our souls. We had probably all hoped that our acts of defiance would be recognised, but what we met was hate and ridicule. We were treated as traitors of the Fatherland.

Everywhere Ludwig went he was seen as a coward, and he heard it so many times that eventually he began to believe it himself. The post-war Germans did not need people like Ludwig Baumann, Helmut Kober or Peter Schilling to remind them of their misdeeds. Hitler's comrades in arms had almost overnight been changed into the children of the new Chancellor Konrad Adenauer's economic wonder; hence there was no time for shame or self-criticism. The deserters were simply an irritating element and their presence a nuisance.

Just like Ludwig, Peter would have expected a post-war life without smears and vilification. But, that was what they all got. For many years they would have to keep struggling. Peter's search for freedom, equality and social justice – the virtues he had been looking for all the time – did not end with the war. It would continue. On his way he had met many Communists, had been inspired by them, and he now decided to look somewhere else for the justice he could not find in the new Federal Republic. The obvious choice of destination was the young Communist state that had been established in the Soviet zone of occupation. Therefore, in 1955, after a short career as a journalist, Peter left for East Germany.

This new search for a fair society could, however, have only one outcome: after having found that a new ruling class had taken over where the Nazis had left, another dream was in tatters. Amidst great need and even hunger, those who filled the power vacuum lacked nothing when it came to luxury. They, the new rulers, had literally taken over everything left behind by the Brownshirts. Behind the Nazis' huge desks one would now find new occupiers, the so-called socialists.

Peter stayed for three years, working in a children's home, but his dream society had let him down. And he was not alone in that opinion. 'They are red-painted Nazis,' a former Communist he had met during the war said, as they met again by chance. This man also had lost his enthusiasm. Once more, Peter decided to flee. He left shortly before the Berlin Wall would have made one more escape practically impossible.

Disillusioned but not finished, Peter looked for a new way. One day he would find it, a way of his own making, a way free of imposed ideologies and teachings. As he said, just as Nazism was identical with mass murder and gas chambers, he could now no longer separate Communism from what was being done in its name. For him all of it, including the Christian Church, was nothing but hypocrisy. He had had enough of it all, and I can hardly blame him.

'When I see all these memorials all over the country in memory of all those who died for their Fatherland, I cannot help thinking that they are there to hide the fact that these men died a miserable death for a criminal cause.' – Ludwig Baumann.

Longing for a hug

'Maybe my father also saw desertion as an act of cowardice,' Ludwig Baumann said as, fifty-five years after the end of the Second World War, we sat in his cosy flat in Bremen-Vegesack and talked about the horrifying years that had not only ruined his youth but had gone on to dominate the rest of his life:

> We did not have a close relationship. He simply could not express emotion. I now had to prove to him that I had changed, that I had become a decent man, ready to live a responsible life. I had done what I thought was right, not only during but also before the war. I had gone my own way, and I think that was a great tragedy for my father. I think it was a tragedy that we never hugged each other. He simply could not manage an embrace, and I most probably did not have such a need at that time. Both of us had suffered immensely, so it was a pity that we couldn't share our feelings openly with each other.

Ludwig's father, who suffered as a result of his son's fate, died shortly after the end of the war. His son now became dependent on alcohol, and in his new role as a businessman (he had taken over his father's company) he managed poorly. In a society where deserters from the conflict were seen as cowards and traitors, it was indeed difficult to exist. Ludwig had survived the war, but in his mind he was finished, a total wreck. He felt alone, discarded, and had every good reason to feel so. Consequently he sought comfort in the bottle, and through alcohol he escaped from it all, or at least he tried to.

Spending many a night in a beer cellar in Hamburg's Gänsemarkt, he soon squandered the inheritance from his father. During the day he drank heavily and at night in his dreams he heard the constant clanking of chains. Ludwig had hoped that after the war his acts and those of his comrades would at least be understood if not commended. But everywhere in society he found Hitler's old cronies, and deserters were scum and traitors in their eyes. On one occasion he looked for a job in the public sector, but, as he says, 'The state didn't want people like me.'

After three years the money had gone. Ludwig slept here and there, surviving by selling curtains. He rang on doors wherever he saw a need, and that was how he met his future wife in Bremen in 1951. She was twelve years younger and lived with her parents. Ludwig and Waltraud soon got married, and children started to arrive, but a stable family life was missing. Ludwig could not stop drinking, and his wife was unhappy. He felt increasingly guilty, and it did not help that he was alone with his tormenting memories. Deserters from the war were not mentioned; they themselves kept quiet; the subject was taboo.

'Throughout our history, soldiers have always been abused and made to destroy – foreign countries and their people, their own country and its people, and, not least, themselves. And afterwards nobody could ever tell what wrong those they had killed had ever done to them. It's all a madness: if I killed somebody on my own, they would call me a murderer; when they tell me to kill him, I am a hero.'

Ludwig Baumann

The stains of shame still haunted the 'traitors' long after Hitler was gone, and, if possible, one would not have admitted to having been a deserter. There were very few who broke that silence. One of them was an author, Alfred Andersch, who confessed his acts in an autobiography, *Die Kirschen der Freiheit* (The Cherries of Freedom), in the early fifties. Andersch openly told how he had deserted from the *Wehrmacht* in Italy in 1944. But this was not popular and he was heavily criticised. Many will have learned a lesson from that, and Andersch's frankness remained an exception. Silence was the norm.

Chapter 18

Business as Usual

On 8 May 1945, the Second World War in Europe concluded with unconditional German capitulation. Peter Schilling and Ludwig Baumann no longer needed to fear Hitler's judges; they no longer needed to fear being sacrificed as cannon-fodder in a penal battalion. However, even after the Third Reich ceased to exist, some of its war judges continued to work as usual. For months after the capitulation, they carried on as if nothing had happened, sentencing German military personnel to death and making sure that the executions were carried out; they continued to murder their compatriots.

This, of course, could not have happened without the implicit consent of those now in charge, the victorious Allied forces. It has been documented that Canadian troops not only closed their eyes to what was going on but in fact delivered weapons to the executioners. Without this help, German troops, who had already been disarmed, would not have been able to carry out these late sentences.

The war was definitely not over for everybody, and certainly not for the sailors Fritz Wehrmann, Martin Schilling and Alfred Gail, who on 9 May, the day after the surrender, were sentenced to death for desertion by still active German military judges. Comrades hung weights to their bodies and threw them overboard after they had been executed aboard the *Buéa* in Geltinger Bay. These three men were no exceptions – there were many others. On 11 May 1945, a firing squad in Flensburg-Mürwik executed Pte Süss after he had been sentenced to death for *Wehrkraftzersetzung*. Süss had commented negatively on an order from one of his non-commissioned officers, and for this offence he had to pay with his life, despite the fact that the war was over.

As late as several months after the end of the war, the Nazi navy still had functioning war courts due to a special mission given to it by the Allies. They had been tasked with removing mines from the sea, and for this purpose specially built ships were still under German command. In the area around Schleswig-Holstein over 750 cases were handled by these still active Nazi judges between 10 May and 5 August 1945. In 424 of these cases, the charge was either unpermitted leave of duty or desertion.

No one has ever been made to pay for this miscarriage of justice – neither those who allowed it to happen nor those judges involved. Only Adolf Hozwig came close, at least, to a slap on the wrist. After the capitulation, he had sentenced three men to death for desertion, and they were all executed. A post-war Hamburg court initially sentenced him to two years imprisonment for this deed, but he was later acquitted on appeal, as no 'intentional misuse of the [Nazi] law' (*Rechtsbeugung*) could be proven in his case. The legal expert advising this court was another former war judge. We have heard about him before: Erich Schwinge.

Schwinge is probably the most infamous of all these Nazi war judges. However, in post-war West Germany, other former Hitlerite lawyers reached greater national prominence, largely due to successful political careers. One of the most famous post-war politicians with Nazi law connections was Hans Filbinger. He served as a member of the conservative Christian Democratic Union (CDU) far into the 1970s, holding various high positions. He was vice-chair of the federal CDU, Minister President of his home state of Baden-Württemberg and, not least, Speaker of the *Bundesrat* (the second parliamentary chamber, equivalent to the House of Lords). The latter position is the fourth highest political post in Germany, preceded only by the President (the Head of State), President of the *Bundestag* (equivalent to the Speaker of the House of Commons) and the Chancellor (the Prime Minister).

As a marine lawyer, Filbinger, a member of the Nazi party since 1937, was to play a crucial part in a number of controversial cases against German seamen, all the way up to the last days of the Third Reich. On 17 April 1945, he sentenced an officer to death in absentia for having fled to Sweden with fourteen of his men. As the Third Reich was crumbling, Filbinger declared that such a deed had undermined morale. However, more than any other, one case in particular would come back to haunt this blood judge – the killing of Walter Gröger.

Walter's mother Anna was a strong opponent of the Nazi movement long before they came to power, and she stayed faithful to her views all her life, even more so after the Nazis and Filbinger had murdered her only son. Mrs Gröger lived with her family in a small village, and that was not easy in times of growing hatred against anybody who would not toe the line of the new rulers. As an unambiguous and unwavering opponent to Hitler, she very quickly found herself without friends. In fact, she had only one co-

Hans Filbinger in 1978.

defender of decency and love of all mankind in the small community, and that was the vicar. This man, no doubt a truthful defender of real Christian values, had banned Brownshirts in his church – obviously convinced he could not convert them. That would soon have consequences: the vicar disappeared without notice, was never heard of again, and a new preacher of the gospel, obviously of a more embracing nature, arrived. From now on, the alleged virtues of the Third Reich would also be included in the sermons; things would be back to normal.

On the day when even Anna's husband came home dressed in a brown uniform, this strong woman had suddenly had enough and a vehement domestic brawl ensued. At the end of the confrontation, Anna, extremely unwisely as far as her own safety was concerned, burned the Nazi costume in her backyard. It was not long after that episode that the war started and Anna finally had to realise that she was powerless against the evil. She had to watch both her husband and son leave for the war, one to the Eastern Front, the other to the German navy.

I do not know what happened to her husband, but from then on, and for the next three years, the mother and her daughters received regular letters in which Walter described one horrible experience after another. When he eventually came home on leave, it was a severely traumatised son that Anna would embrace at her door. For him it had been nothing but blood, death and terror. And it was not just the dangers of battle; it was about being treated like a slave, constantly exposed to the most severe harassment. Walter asked himself how it could be that if somebody wanted to win a war with somebody else, he would treat that person as nothing but shit. Whilst on leave, according to later family accounts, Walter kept waking up at night, drenched in sweat. He told them of the horror of the war, of his young friends, some not much more than children, jumping ship while burning like torches.

'What once was right can't be wrong today'

The days at home were few; soon Walter had to go back to the horrors, and thereafter there were no more letters. The next the family would hear from him did not come from Walter himself but from a *Wehrmacht* prison in Norway. Pte Gröger, so it was alleged, had not returned from a short leave he had been granted, and the family was now told of the consequence of that offence for the young man.

This is what was later revealed about these events: Walter had met Marie Lindgren, a young Norwegian, who had invited him home. Marie's brother worked as an undercover smuggler of refugees, and it was now planned that Walter would be helped to escape to Sweden. However, before anything further happened, the brother was arrested and the Gestapo subsequently found Walter in Marie's home. The next step was a war court.

At first, Walter was lucky: the judge sentenced him to only eight years. However, it was not to stop there. The sentence was disapproved of by the admiral; he requested a death sentence. And this is where the future CDU politician enters the stage. In Oslo, on 16 January 1945, Walter was tried again and this time Marine Judge Filbinger acted as prosecutor. During the trial, he smeared Marie Lindgren with words like 'pig' and 'spy' and, as expected, Filbinger got his way. Walter was sentenced to death and was executed at Akershus fortress in Oslo on 16 March – only two hours after the sentence had been handed down and just weeks before the end of the war. For whatever reason, Filbinger had been extremely eager to push forward with the execution. He even appointed himself to be the leading officer at the execution, the one overseeing the process.

This might have been the end of the story, as it was with so many others, but that was not the case. What happened during and immediately after this trial would, years later, come back to haunt the prosecuting judge. It took a few years, but Walter's case did in the end damage Filbinger's reputation at least, if nothing else. Eventually, in 1978, as a result of media pressure, he had to withdraw from public service. Yet the honorary chairmanship of his party in Baden-Württemberg was not withdrawn, and he was never brought to trial. Powerful politicians guaranteed that.

Hans Filbinger was never in real danger, no matter what was disclosed about his past. He was too important a person for his party colleagues. They did everything they could to defend him. In 1981, Helmut Kohl made his stance perfectly clear: 'The libel campaign against Hans Filbinger is without comparison in the history of the republic. We must all be ready to learn from the bitter experiences of this witch hunt.' An earlier president of the Federal Constitutional Court, Professor Gerhard Müller, was also full of compassion: 'A tremendous injustice has been done toward Hans Filbinger that is not possible to undo or compensate for.'

But these powerful voices were only examples of the unwavering support that the former Nazi judge received from his political friends as he continued to fight for his reputation. The party stood by him and, as late as 2 June 1995, the press office of the CDU/CSU Conservative political union declared:

> It cannot be right that fifty years after the war they will now succeed in doing what Hitler failed to do – making the whole machinery of war justice an instrument of Nazi terror. We will not give in and do all these men a further injustice, those who for fifty years were put in the Nazi corner by the Stasi, Wolf and company [the East German Secret Service and its leader]. This especially goes for Hans Filbinger.

His own words at this point were: 'What once was right can't be wrong today.'

It could be said about the Filbinger affair that it was less about what he had done and more about how years later he defended himself and how he was defended by his political colleagues. 'What had been right then was right now.' The most senior German politicians, all those years later, still therefore saw Nazi justice as legitimate law passed by a legitimate regime. This was their opinion on the matter, so there was no reason for Filbinger or any of the other former judges to fear prosecution.

The judge who presided at the trial of Pte Johann Scholtyssek was no exception. The twenty-four-year-old soldier had appeared in front of one of Filbinger's colleagues after a personal tragedy. When he returned from the front in 1942, his wife had found a lover. Hurt and angry, the soldier made a critical remark about the Führer's war. His father-in-law reported him to the authorities and Scholtyssek was soon arrested and, together with forty-four other prisoners, taken on a lorry to Münster, where he was prosecuted by a special court.

The sentences here as elsewhere were passed in assembly-line fashion, and after twenty minutes it was all over, for all of them. For several days Scholtyssek lay in shackles awaiting execution, before being pardoned and moved to the concentration camp at Esterwegen. From there, he was later transferred to Calais as a forced labourer. Many of his fellow prisoners committed suicide, but he struggled through. He was strong and had a mission: 'I wanted to go after the old geezer who had turned me in,' he said. However, that never did happen. 'Once I succeeded in getting to talk to him, he legged it to the police, who immediately arrested me.'

Scholtyssek's father-in-law never had to face responsibility for his actions; nor did the judge who, dismissing anything the emotionally traumatised private had to say, simply consigned him to death. Yet it was Scholtyssek, not they, who was considered an ex-convict for the rest of his life.

Chapter 19

Whitewash in Persil

At the Potsdam Conference after the end of the war, the three victorious powers agreed on fundamental principles for the treatment of post-war Germany. Important articles in the agreement that ended the conference were demilitarisation, decentralisation, democratisation and denazification.

Here we will concentrate on the latter. It was decided that the denazification programme was to be carried out by each of the four occupying powers in their respective zone of responsibility. Soon this devolvement of roles would result in very different ways of dealing with the Nazis, particularly between the three western zones and the zone controlled by the Soviet Union.

In the Soviet zone, in what was to develop into the German Democratic Republic (East Germany), denazification was connected with an economic rebuilding according to Communist principles. As a result, half a million people with (or allegedly with) Nazi connections were removed from their posts between 1945 and 1947, and replaced with people loyal to the new ruling party. However, not only Nazi criminals were excluded and/or detained as politically unwelcome citizens in the Communist zone (and later state). Democratic opponents of the SED, the East German Communist regime, were also among these people. This mix of two disparate groups would come to play a major role, years later, in the controversial struggle for rehabilitation of the victims of Nazi war tribunals. We will return to that later.

At this point it is important to stress that the GDR in general did remove people with Nazi connections from all sectors of public life and did put them on trial. From 1945 to 1964, 16,572 individuals were charged with war crimes and crimes against peace and humanity. Of those brought to trial, 12,807 were found guilty and 1,578 were acquitted. In 2,187 cases, the process was discontinued, as the accused was either absent or dead. Of those found guilty, 118 were sentenced to death and 231 to life imprisonment.

The denazification programme was initially thoroughly carried out also in the American zone, but in a slightly different manner. However, things suddenly changed; the US stopped the programme at the beginning of the Cold War and, on 31 March 1948, court cases against the worst perpetrators, all far from completed, were adjourned. Thus, many people with a dark and criminal past escaped punishment; they were never brought to justice.

The British and French viewed the issue of denazification first and foremost from a pragmatic perspective, and for them it was more important to rebuild public services and private businesses than to charge Nazis with crimes against humanity. This lack of interest in making war criminals pay for their crimes led to the introduction of a special system that would clear the way for Hitler's cronies. They needed to possess a document that verified that the holder had neither held any questionable position in society during the Nazi period nor had been a volunteer member of any Nazi organisation. This document was issued by a special office under the denazification authorities and was colloquially referred to as a *Persilschein* (Persil certificate) after the well-known washing powder. The reality was that those with a dubious past often only needed another person who was not a Nazi to vouch for them. That was often how easy it was to wipe the slate clean. Here it might be suitable to remember the fate of Ludwig Baumann and note the difference.

> On 1 December 1949, only three months after the Federal Republic had been established, an amnesty law, 'Law on Granting of Impunity', was passed by the new West German parliament, the *Bundestag*. The so-called desk criminals, Nazi officials who with a stroke of a pen had wiped out the lives of hundreds of thousands of human beings, would from now mostly be left in peace.

Many Nazis got 'Persil certificates' and few were ever punished. Those who got off most lightly were often those who had committed the worst crimes, and there are several examples that speak for themselves. We have already heard of Hans Filbinger, but he was just one, albeit one of the most famous. Another post-war politician with a problematic background was Theodor Oberländer.

Oberländer was a member of the *Bundestag* from 1953 to 1960, and served as a minister in the Adenauer government. But he had also had a military career, and not one of the most heroic. Major Oberländer, a Nazi who had held a number of different public positions in Hitler's party, had also been the commander of the so-called 'Nightingale' unit. During the war, these soldiers committed atrocious crimes against the civilian population in invaded countries. One of these murderous events took place on 30 June 1941 in the Soviet town of Lvov. Between three and five thousand people were murdered by Oberländer's men on this day alone. But Lvov was just one of many targets for the future Adenauer minister, and in this activity there had been no place for second thoughts: members of the unit who refused to participate in the mass liquidations were themselves killed. At one point Oberländer had seven of his people court-martialled and executed in one single action. This man became a post-war minister for refugees …

'They had acted … in good faith'

While the Nazis were given 'Persil certificates' and climbed back onto their career ladders, almost everything was done to delegitimise the resistance movement. In the mid-fifties, this defamation campaign still included the men connected with the 20 July assassination plot. However, there were attempts to look into what had really happened after von Stauffenberg's botched assassination attempt. Who had been right? Who had been wrong? Had the men who had taken part in the plotting been lawfully executed or murdered outright?

In June 1956, this process had reached the country's highest court; the judge and prosecutor involved in the mock trial that led to the execution of six of the conspirators, among them Bonhoeffer, were tried by the West German Supreme Court. It had been an achievement to get that far, but for those on the resistance fighters' side it ended in disappointment.

The final ruling was, to say the least, remarkable. The judge, Otto Thorbeck, was acquitted; he was seen as having done nothing wrong. However, Walter Huppenkothen, the Nazi prosecutor, was found guilty and sentenced to six years in prison for his role in the mock trial. Had Huppenkothen been made a scapegoat for the murders, while the judge got off scot free, though the latter had made the final decisions? Not really; the prosecutor was punished because the death sentences had not been properly confirmed and because he, as the prosecutor in the case, and therefore against the rules, had been present at the executions.

Huppenkothen was accused of, and sentenced for, these two procedural errors, not for having called for the killing of these men. Therefore we can conclude that the Federal Supreme Court, eleven years after the war, had decided that the conspirators had been lawfully sentenced and executed by a proper court of law for having opposed Hitler and the Nazi regime. The reason for that decision was, and we have heard this before, that 'according to the existing laws at the time, whose legality there is no reason to question, the actions of the resistance fighters had fulfilled what was required in order for the judge to rule that they had committed treason'.

The court also made it clear that, due to the resistance people and their activities, unnecessary blood of German soldiers had been sacrificed. 'The opposition had taken upon themselves a great responsibility,' it was declared. The final message was that the summary court in Flossenbürg had had no other choice than to sentence these people to death:

> When it comes down to the basic question of a state's own existence, all governments at all times have issued severe laws to protect themselves. They [the judge and prosecutor] had acted according to the law and in good faith.

Once again the Nazi judicial system – and, by extension, the Hitler government – was declared legitimate and its judges exculpated. It is interesting to note who passed such a verdict in 1956. Of the five judges on the panel, four of them – Max Hörchner, Ludwig Peetz, Ludwig Martin and Ernst Mantel – had been judges and prosecutors in the service of the Third Reich.

Let us have a look at the history of one of them. Ernst Mantel had not been a member of the Nazi party but had loyally served the regime in all its doing. From 1934, he served the Nazis at the People's Court (*Volksgerichtshof*), the infamous Nazi court system for political cases. After being promoted in 1940 to the legal department of the highest command of the army, Mantel worked closely with his new line manager, Lt Gen. Eugen Müller.

After the Soviet Union was attacked, these two men's duty included making sure that all supreme commanders of the army had sworn to follow the so-called Commissary Order. This order called upon all soldiers of the *Wehrmacht* to shoot without trial any commissary of the Soviet army and not treat them as prisoners of war. In 1945, Mantel was promoted to general judge, and from then on his responsibility was to assess applications for pardon from sentenced soldiers.

All this was documented and well known, but it constituted no problem when Mantel continued his career after the war. He was not even an exceptional case: among the forty or so Supreme Court judges at the time Mantel was there, twenty-seven had a background as lawyers serving the Nazi state. Now we understand why Bonhoeffer's murderers were let off the hook.

From this time, or shortly after, the West German population would have been aware of the presence of these influential men who again dominated the country. The publication that revealed it all in the early 1960s came from East Germany. Walter Ulbricht's researchers had suitably called it the 'Brown Book', but it was not welcome reading in Bonn and was dismissed as Communist propaganda. But what it told, and what has since been further documented, is that the criminals got away with it.

Men of 'honour'

'Brown Book' or not, in West Germany people did not want to know too much; they wanted to forget, and there were thousands of influential individuals who happily agreed: many had a considerable personal interest in sweeping it all under the carpet, and so it was.

As we have seen, the war courts were regarded as having been a guarantee for justice and were beyond reproach. But, as in the case of Ernst Mantel, not even having a past as a judge in the service of the infamous People's Courts would ruin a future career as a lawyer in post-war West Germany.

The People's Court had been a special court system established in 1934, shortly after the Nazis had come to power. These courts worked outside of the normal legal system and specialised in political offences. Such crimes could have included almost anything and were summed up in the now for us familiar *Wehrkraftzersetzung* – basically anything that would go against the ruling party. The offenders were punished severely, with the death penalty in thousands of cases; justice was not the priority in the work of these special courts, and, even less, compassion. The judges did most of the work themselves: they accused, incriminated and vilified the defendants and passed whatever sentence they saw fit, all this without much objection from whoever had been appointed as defence counsel. These court proceedings in no way remotely lived up to what would be expected from a judicial system in a constitutional state. They were mock courts where normal principles of law and justice were completely disregarded. All that was acknowledged after the war, but it made no difference to the future of all these judges who during the Hitler years had happily operated with a blood-stained dagger hidden under their robes.

When the war ended, there were approximately 570 judges and prosecutors attached to this system of perverted justice, and none was ever held responsible for his actions. Instead of facing prosecution themselves, these people continued in successful careers within the West German post-war legal system. A ruling by the Federal Supreme Court (*Bundesgerichtshof*) in 1956 indicates with the greatest clarity that this was no mistake; the judges at the highest court of the country fully supported their Nazi colleagues and declared that those lawyers who had been part of the People's Court system should be granted what came to be known as the 'Judges' Privilege'. This decision would finally safeguard any of them from possible prosecution. The basis for the ruling was that their actions had been legal at the time, i.e. under the rules of the Third Reich.

Among men who benefited from this generosity were Paul Reimers, who continued as a regional court judge in Ravensburg; Hans-Dietrich Arndt, who became chief judge at the Supreme Court of the state of Rheinland-Pfalz in Koblenz; Robert Bandel, who carried on as chief district judge in Kehl; Andreas Fricke, who was appointed as a judge in Brunswick, and Erich Hammel, who until 1964 led the North Rhine-Westphalia Supreme Court in Duisburg. Many, but not all, continued in public service: numerous Hitlerite lawyers went on to practise law as independent professionals. Georg Zippel (an early convert, with Nazi membership No. 1,553,525) continued in a successful private career in Bonn, and, had I ever needed legal advice myself, as I once lived in the state of Hesse, I could have got it from the old Nazi Ernst Wildberger nearby. Wildberger had joined Hitler's party in 1933 and after the war had been allowed to advise others about democratic law in Fulda.

The list is long; these are only a few examples. They all got away with it. Or just about – one of these judges was to some extent held responsible. Public Prosecutor Ernst Lautz was sentenced to ten years' imprisonment by a US military tribunal. However, after only four years, he was pardoned and granted a government pension for his loyal service to the state.

One of the worst of these men we have already met, but let us look at what became of him. Not surprisingly, Erich Schwinge was also allowed to continue practising law. In 1946, in Marburg, he was appointed as dean at the university and professor of what he knew best – military law. The fact that Himmler himself had once found one of Schwinge's sentences unreasonably harsh was clearly no hindrance. From that day, Schwinge was not only back as a renowned and respected expert in military justice, besides his duties at the university and his part-time job as legal adviser to the government in Bonn (yes, true), he also acted as defence lawyer in about 150 cases against war criminals.

Schwinge was a busy man, but he also found time to campaign in defence of the Nazi armed forces and their legal systems. In that capacity he not only wrote a number of short articles but finished off a major report on the work of the military courts during the Third Reich. *Die deutsche Militärjustiz in der Zeit des Nationalsozialismus* (German Military Justice during the Nazi Era) was finally published in 1978 and for a long time thereafter this book was recognised as the standard work on this matter. Originally the renowned Institute of Contemporary History (*Institut für Zeitgeschichte*) in Munich had asked the former chief prosecutor and air force judge Otto Peter Schweling to write the book. As a military lawyer, Schweling had worked as senior prosecutor for the Federal Prosecution during the war. He accepted the commission, but when he presented his work in 1966, the institute refused to publish it because they found the style too apologetic. After that, almost ten years passed before anything happened to the manuscript. Schweling was now dead and out of the picture, and in came Schwinge. Out of Schweling's original script, Schwinge completed an even more apologetic work with emphasis on the following 'truth':

> The armed forces and the Nazis were natural contrasts. A *modus vivendi* existed between them, and the armed forces did not look for conflict as, according to their principles, they were not prepared for political struggle.

The book came to be highly regarded, but it was evident that it perverted the truth. Though there had not been much justice in Nazi law, and definitely not within the military jurisdiction, the field in which the two men had been active, Schweling and Schwinge had tried their best to present a picture of a perfectly fair and morally correct system. They claimed:

> The war judges acted with restraint, care and leniency [...] The sentences they meted out might have been harsh, but they certainly held themselves within the limits of the jurisdiction, not only according to the prevailing view of the time but also in line with what can be expected by a democratic constitutional state.

Though it was their opinion that the war had been about defending the country and Europe against the Communists, and that unpleasant methods had therefore been a 'military necessity', they stressed that 'German war justice, despite the need for unity in face of the Bolsheviks, never degraded itself to become a blind tool for draconian laws'. Or, as Schwinge pointed out as his strongest argument: 'Hitler didn't like the war judges, as they were too kind.'

As one of these kind and compassionate judges, Schwinge was elected in the early 1950s as deputy chairman of the Liberals, the FDP, in the state of Hesse. He also became a deeply involved and outspoken member of the network of former war judges that had been established in order to support and help any colleague who was in trouble. In the first twenty years or so of post-war West Germany this loosely organised network provided general help and legal assistance to any comrade who was exposed to criticism or scrutiny of his past as a Hitlerite judge. The members also collected money and provided support for relatives of fellow judges who were still held in prisoner-of-war camps, and they helped those who chose not to go back to work to retire with good pensions. The network of men met regularly to discuss how to deal with any threat to their professional group's reputation, and, in all of this, Schwinge was one of the most outspoken and influential members.

For the lawyers, this ongoing work was of immense importance; it was needed in order to block any judicial and/or political attempt to make themselves responsible for their involvement during the war. But it was also about the future; many of these men had an interest in getting back to work in their own speciality – as military judges. Unfortunately for them, this did not happen. The establishment of a new military court system would take much longer than it had after the end of the First World War. When it finally happened, in 2013, these people were long dead. For Schwinge it was much too late; he never saw his dream come true.

Chapter 20

Meeting a Dutch War Criminal

From 1962 and until his death some forty years later, Peter Schilling, who became a song writer and performer, lived in the Netherlands and earned his living as a court interpreter. He was a free man, finally living his own life. However, even here his past would catch up with him.

On 9 May 1977, the trial of Pieter Menten, Holland's most well-known Nazi war criminal, was to begin, and Peter had been appointed as interpreter. Peter was now in his fifties, but he would come to realise that the Nazis were still out there; they had not gone away. They had come to haunt him again.

Before the war, Pieter Menten, a Dutch businessman of dubious nature, had moved to the Free City of Danzig (today Gdańsk in Poland) and made himself a millionaire. Apart from that, he also served as the Dutch consul of Kraków and made important friends, people who would mean a lot for his future career. After the outbreak of war, the businessman changed path. Menten joined the Security Police (*Sicherheitspolizei*) SiPo-SD, the ideologically trained special forces set up to commit mass murder in the east, and rose quickly in their ranks. The extermination of Jews, Communists and others started as soon as the German army entered the Soviet Union, and the Dutchman played an important and leading role in these extensive killings. One witness recalled, years after the events:

> When the executions took place here in 1941, I was eleven years old. But I still remember it all, as if it was only yesterday. Menten was in command; he ordered everyone in the village, including children, to come and watch the killings. He didn't shoot anybody himself, but each time the order was given by him.

This last remark was consistent with other witness observations from elsewhere: Menten did not shoot anyone himself, but he was the leader.

> I can still very vividly see them walk the plank over the dug-out mass grave. As they were shot, they fell right down into the prepared grave. The commands were given by Menten. On that day, 7 July, only men were killed. But on 28 August it was the women's and children's turn.

Apart from ordering and overseeing the murder of unwanted people, Menten developed another interest: he became the 'administrator of Jewish antiques and art collections', i.e. he started to track down art treasurers for the benefit of the Third Reich, becoming one of Hitler's most high-profile art robbers. However, the spoils from these thefts must have gone into his own pockets as well. After the war, the former Nazi officer, now one of the richest men in Holland, lived an untroubled life in a house crammed with treasures of dubious origin. Only after the journalist Hans Knopp started to look into Menten's past, thirty years after the end of the war, did the wealthy art collector's background become known to his Dutch compatriots.

Smelling trouble, the old Nazi fled to Switzerland, knowing that the Alpine country twenty-five years earlier had protected him from being brought to justice in Poland. This time, however, the Swiss changed their mind, and following an extradition request from Holland, Menten was sent back to his homeland to face justice. This is where Pieter Menten's and Peter Schilling's paths were to cross.

During the war, some Jews had hidden in an attic in Amsterdam, and one of them, a man named Hauptmann, was presented as a prosecution witness in the trial. Years after, Peter remembered this man's testimony with the utmost clarity. According to Mr Hauptmann, he had seen from the attic window his own sister showing some papers to SS Officer Menten, most probably the visa documents for the US she had just received for herself and her children. Menten gave a sign to one of his men with a machine gun, the sister and her children then moved out of sight, and a volley of machine-gun fire could be heard. Mr Hauptmann never saw his sister and her children again.

Thereafter this testimony was portrayed in a lengthy speech as nothing but complete fantasy by an expert witness called by the defence, a lawyer from Düsseldorf, Mr Hartlich. This was the point when the past caught up with the interpreter and made him lose his professional neutrality. While simultaneously interpreting what amounted to nothing but a Nazi rant, Peter started to feel increasingly uneasy and indisposed.

'Jews' testimonies are untrustworthy,' the expert witness declared, and Peter's translation got increasingly incoherent and shaky. Past and present started to get totally mixed up in his mind.

'My own ordeals came to life. For an interpreter in court, that is not allowed; one is not supposed to get personally involved in the subject.' Consequently, Peter had no choice; he got up from his chair, apologised and asked for permission to leave. 'I am not able to continue,' he said. The judge thought the complexity of the translation had caused his problem and declared a short break. However, Peter explained that there was another reason why he could not continue; he was unable to fulfil what was expected of him.

Having had to leave in this way in front of the international media, in the midst of what was probably the biggest war crime trial the Netherlands had ever seen, Peter felt humiliated; he felt a total failure. In the foyer, two security guards came over to him. 'What is it, De heer Schilling?' they asked. 'Are you also a Jew, since it affected you so much?' Peter was shaking, but '... with great effort I managed to whisper "Bloody hell, does one need to be a Jew, Russian or whatever to be a victim of them?"'

Mr Hauptman, the man who had lost his family in such a brutal way, had had a very good memory. His testimony had brought the horrors back to the interpreter. However, Peter could manage that. What he could not manage was the Nazi defence presented by the German expert witness. 'It must have been the sarcastic tone that did me in. It was like the sharp, cutting voice of Joseph Goebbels.'

Menten was found guilty and sentenced to fifteen years in prison. This verdict was annulled on a technicality and a re-trial followed. The final sentence was passed in 1980, and it ended with a ten-year term behind bars for having murdered Jewish villagers in 1941. After having served six years, the war criminal was released. He tried to retire to his mansion in Ireland, but as he was refused entry to the country, he had to live his last years in an old people's home in Loosdrecht, Holland.

Chapter 21

Challenging the Establishment

'Then my wife died while giving birth to our sixth child, and suddenly I found myself all alone with full responsibility for the family.' The death of Ludwig Baumann's wife in 1966 was the wake-up call that got him back on his feet. From then on he was left alone to care for the children, and as a result of this pressure he succeeded in freeing himself from his dependence on alcohol. The eldest Baumann child looked after the youngest while Ludwig worked hard to put food on the table.

Another turning point in Ludwig's life was his meeting with the emerging peace and Third World movements, with which he became involved. In addition to caring for his children, Ludwig slowly started to get in touch with a new generation, for whom strict discipline was no longer the most important virtue in life. Among his new friends, a modest and unassuming man like Ludwig was turned into something of a hero, much against his will.

However, outside these circles, which became Ludwig's refuge, deserters were still despised, at least the category he belonged to. Another group had arrived on the stage as well, and with them it was different. The newly arrived were seen in a wholly different light as a result of a new political background. The difference between one deserter and another was clearly evident. Those who came from the former eastern zone, the German Democratic Republic, had escaped from the enemy, the Communists on the other side of the wall, and were automatically treated as heroes.

Ludwig recalled:

The Cold War was at its height. The USA had put up rockets that could decapitate the Soviet Union. They would have been able to hit any target. The Russians, with their big SS20s, felt threatened by a Germany that so few years before had waged a war of annihilation against them. Yes, we were hugely anxious that the Soviet Union would react to this, and therefore hundreds of thousands of people took to the streets to demonstrate against the Cold War. It was in this context that many army reservists withdrew and created the memorial known as 'The Unknown Deserter'. It resulted in a terrible brawl and would lead me back to my past.

The new war resisters and Third World activists had given him courage; they had given him the strength to stand by what he had kept hidden in his mind for over forty years. Slowly the deserter started to free himself from his manacles and straighten his back. Ludwig decided to face his past and fight back.

The memorial 'The Unknown Deserter' was unveiled in April 1986 in a council building in Bremen-Vegesack. At this time, the peace movement was growing strong and, supported by them, for the first time, after decades in hiding, deserters and other victims of the Nazi war courts slowly began to stand up to society's scorn. However, as Ludwig Baumann recalls, 'Every time Bremen Mayor Klaus Wedemeier met with the then minister of defence, Wörner of the CDU, the latter demanded, "That deserter thing has to be removed, otherwise Bremen will not get any more armament assignments"'.

After the fall of the Berlin Wall, the time had finally come. With thirty-five other elderly men and one woman, Ludwig founded the *Bundesvereinigung der Opfer der NS-Militärjustiz* (the Federal Union of Victims of Nazi Military Justice). The chief purpose of the new organisation was to demand that all sentences passed by Nazi war tribunals should be declared invalid – i.e. all victims, whether dead or alive, should be legally rehabilitated without being subjected to any individual conditions. The only woman in the group had served in the Luftwaffe. After the bungled assassination attempt on Hitler, she had uttered: 'Shame it wasn't successful. Had it been, we would soon have peace.' Sentencing her, the judge wrote: 'She must be eradicated.'

To find all these people was in itself a major achievement. Ludwig told me, as we sat in his small, cosy flat in a Bremen suburb fifty-six years after the end of the war:

In one concentration camp they had kept the card indexes of the prisoners. Such records helped us find former deserters. Our first meeting was to become the founding general assembly of the new association. For the first time many of these men could talk about their experiences to another human being. Some had tears in their eyes and were not able to open up. They had suppressed their experiences for so many years and could not just suddenly open the lid on their past.

From that time we have fought for our rehabilitation and the restoration of our dignity. Yes, some would call it honour, but I prefer to call it dignity. We will continue our struggle, not only for ourselves but also for future generations. I feel that desertion should be acknowledged as a human right. I dream about a humane present and future, devoid of all violence.

Therapy to help ease the psychological damage these men had suffered had rarely been an option, Ludwig told me:

> Some victims are obsessed with the past; they can't talk about anything else; others are not able even to broach the subject. Some have grown-up children who can no longer bear to listen, while others have offspring who are and always have been there for their fathers.

This is true of Ludwig's second youngest son. As Ludwig says: 'He has not fully lived his own life but is always there for me.' Among the men in the group there were two others whose sons had been completely devoted to them. However, both these sons had committed suicide, as they could no longer carry the burden or come to terms with the fate of their fathers. This is a tremendous tragedy, but is unfortunately not surprising. As is common with most victims of torture and severe ill-treatment, not only the deserters themselves were victimised, but the whole family were, including the next generation. How suffering can be transferred to children is well documented in literature about torture.

For Hitler's deserters this has been more difficult due to their isolation and society's contempt for them. They had no allies but were left to care for themselves, or, as we have seen in some cases, be cared for by their own vulnerable children. Ludwig himself did not meet one single deserter in all those years before that day when the thirty-six men and one woman arrived for the first meeting of the new association.

The 'brave' general

In 1989, the Federal Government continued to argue in parliament that only in exceptional cases could it be claimed that an injustice had been done when soldiers had been sentenced for desertion during the Second World War. No, they must not be rehabilitated. The background for this statement was that desertion had also been a capital offence for the Allies. This must have been like a slap in the face for the victims. With this argument, the government did not acknowledge the huge difference between an aggressive and a defensive war. They blatantly refused to see the obvious difference between, on the one hand, a criminal regime's oppression and abuse of its youth and, on the other, the precarious situation of democratic states under attack.

There was no end to the injustice. In March 1993, Ludwig Baumann discovered that 128 Latvian mercenaries under the *Waffen-SS* had continued to receive a regular income from the German state, all according to the letter of the law, and that the widow of one of the bloodiest of all blood judges, Roland Freisler, had received a substantial pension for her husband, based on his years as president of the People's Court. These were no isolated cases. The question about pensions is a very painful issue and the pattern was clear. For example, widows of SS officers had received war pensions, while the widows of executed deserters (with one exception, following the Kassel verdict mentioned in the next chapter) had not, and pensions for the surviving deserters had been reduced as a consequence of the missing years spent in prisons and not at the front. For every day they did not march, money was deducted from the pension fund, while those who had served in the SS and other special units had a right to allowances in accordance with length of duty.

During all these years Ludwig had had to struggle against a powerful adversary in the *Ring Deutscher Soldatenverbände*, the German Association of Soldiers. At the time, this organisation represented 430,000 people and their leader was Gen. Jürgen Schreiber, a veteran of the war. According to him, desertion was the gravest of all crimes. Consequently, the Association of Soldiers completely refused to help in the deserters' struggle for rehabilitation, and did everything possible to oppose it.

Schreiber, who saw the deserters as evaders, himself once had to fight for his reputation. Now, many years later, it has been revealed that as an airman during the war, he tried to avoid a duty fraught with danger with the help of personal connections. In February 1945, as the Luftwaffe was under immense pressure, its personnel were commanded to go and reinforce the similarly pressurised infantry. Schreiber sent several letters to his father regarding this matter, letters later found in an archive in Prague. 'Dear father, do something so that I don't have to go to the front,' was the message. The young officer's father was an influential war judge, and his son begged him to 'do something before it is too late'.

It was with that background, which no doubt he would have preferred to have remained hidden, that Schreiber stormed against any attempt to show the deserters even the slightest hint of compassion. For him, as for so many others, the very thought of a blanket rehabilitation of these men would have been a charge against not only the armed forces but a whole generation of soldiers, not least himself. The general had a skeleton in his own cupboard, yet was nonetheless able to target those who had already been badly hurt in both heart and soul.

Many have been happy to defend the myth of the armed forces as innocent and clean, and Schreiber and his friends were merely examples of that. In the political arena, a group of very strong proponents of the same view dominated the issue: the deserters, not the party and its military, had let down their country. 'Every single case has to be tried,' was for years the rallying cry of Norbert Geis, the CSU politician and spokesman on legal matters. According to him, many deserters had committed crimes before their escape and had tried to avoid being punished, and only a few had had political motives. 'This way there will be no Persil certificates for the deserters, as not all of them had political motives.'

In no way would Geis and his party give in. In order to build up his case against any threat, he therefore used experts who he could rely on not to let him down. The former war judge Otfried Keller was one of those; Franz W. Seidler, professor of modern military history at the War College in Munich, was another. Seidler had written a book (*Fahnenflucht*, 1993) in which he stated that most of the deserters had not escaped because they were against the war but because they were afraid of punishment for other offences. 'Their level of education was too low to make such a decision.' According to him, the deserters were mostly simple people who often came from dysfunctional families and had not completed even vocational training. Seidler painted the deserters as inferior and continued on the road laid out by the Nazis, who had likewise stated that these people had been inferior and asocial individuals.

In one particular case, captured deserters had been used as forced labour under sub-human conditions and thousands had consequently died. But, according to the professor, their food supplies had been sufficient and the living conditions more than satisfactory. According to Seidler, those who became ill were personally responsible for their maladies, and the deterioration in the state of health among the prisoners was because many had swapped provisions for tobacco and eaten raw potatoes. As Seidler, who could seek cover for his extraordinary views under his title as professor, was one of the most important experts in the entire rehabilitation process for the victims of war justice, his views were very damaging to the deserters' cause. In Ludwig's opinion: 'This man has trained numerous officers for the defence forces. He totally lacks distance from the Third Reich.'

'Long live the German Reich'

As a deserter, Ludwig Baumann received some disturbing mail over the years:

Honourable association of deserters,

Where do we live? It can only be in a banana republic that an association like yours stands up against the armed forces of the state. Who is it that formed your association? Probably only the kind who have been guilty of desertion, plundering, cowardice, refusal to follow orders, theft from comrades, the rape of women in occupied territories, homosexuality, sabotage, self-mutilation, co-operation with the enemy and other similar crimes.

And now you act as men of resistance to get damages, something that, if you succeed, the participants of the war, those who acted decently and upright till the last day, will have to pay for with their taxes. Deserters like you, Mr Baumann, must understand that desertion within all armies in the world is punished by death when it takes place in wartime. There are no other ways to deal with such cowards who let down their comrades to save their own arses. Put them up against the wall or cut their throats! That is the right thing to do with such creatures who lack character, conscience or comradeship.

Everyone wanted to survive the war, but millions nevertheless did their duty till the bitter end. Sure, only a few of them were connected to the Nazi regime. Nevertheless, they remained loyal and decent to the last day, with the conviction that they should defend the soil of their Fatherland. However, it is absolutely disgraceful that executed deserters, traitors of their comrades, are given memorials. It shows contempt for those who kept their honour in the war and lost their lives. But, as they say, in present-day

Germany everything is possible.

This letter was anonymous, as was the card carrying the following message: 'I can only regret that you were not shot or beheaded. In my eyes you and the other miserable scum are beneath contempt. You are murderers who let your comrades down.'

But there were exceptions; some people would happily give both name and address. In March 1994, Alois Groeblehner, a former lieutenant colonel in the air force, had even copied in pictures, one of himself and one of the Führer.

Mr Baumann,

From the German media I have heard that you, as a deserter, have been given permission to speak at *Volkstrauertag* [People's Mourning Day, a public holiday in Germany]. In this Fettered Remains of Germany [FRG, Federal Republic of Germany] nothing is any longer impossible. However, Mr Vermin Baumann, you can be sure that you shall be held responsible by the Reich War Court in Berlin. The German Reich is still at war and therefore war justice still applies.

What is best for you now is to take cyanide. That will salve your frayed nerves and will spare you an encounter with the Reich justice system, which will soon be operating again, and will save the state quite a few Reichmark.

The letter from Alois Groeblehner to Ludwig Baumann.

Always loyal to German justice and the truth, I remain faithful to the oath with the words: Long live the German Reich.

With German greetings,

Alois Groeblehner

The senders differed, but the message was almost always the same.

Chapter 22

Seeking the Truth

Ludwig was close to despair. He had just spoken as one of the experts at a hearing by the law committee of the *Bundestag*, and now he had to endure listening to a former military judge, Otfried Keller, defending and justifying himself and his old colleagues. Keller, who after the war served as president of the Supreme Court of the state of Hesse, not only claimed that Hitler's war courts had operated in a way that was fully consistent with what a constitutional state would expect of them, but the procedures had, according to him, 'been a blessing'. However, it was not only Ludwig who struggled to control himself. The Green Party representative, Christa Nickels, was also extremely upset about Keller's statements and exclaimed: 'It is unbelievable; he defends the Nazi judges!'

Yes, he did; in fact, he was one of them himself, and he had no regrets. According to Keller, there was nothing to criticise in the Nazi legal system. 'That was the law at the time,' he asserted. And this view was supported by other expert witnesses who had also been called upon to give their statements, as part of the committee's preparatory work on a deserters' rehabilitation bill.

Schreiber also stood firm and said: 'Any recruit will at any time learn that being absent from the troops is a crime and will be punished,' adding that the war judges had had nothing to do with the Nazi system. According to him, this could be proven by the fact that Adolf Hitler never invited a war judge to come and see him. Something similar was expressed by Seidler: 'Hitler did not give a damn about the war judges. They were too lax and apolitical.' For Ludwig, personal memories and the huge number of barbaric sentences told another story. It was not easy for him to listen to these people.

As was clearly shown at this hearing, for decades after the war there had been enormous opposition to justice for the deserters. However, we must not forget that support had also been building up. For many years, until his death in 1999, Ignatz Bubis was chairman of *Zentralrat der Juden in Deutschland* (the Central Council of Jews in Germany). Bubis, a renowned advocate for co-operation, forgiveness and justice, had strong opinions about this issue:

> I understand and support the demand for rehabilitation and damages for the deserters. These people must not be seen as criminals, but must be honoured for their conviction. There must be a general rehabilitation without any reservations for all war resisters and other victims of war justice, not only the survivors. Yes, it must also

encompass the dead. Of course, it will affect more than those directly concerned, as it will make clear that resistance against a dictatorial regime of terror and refusal to follow its orders must not be punished but be given due respect. I don't see any danger that rehabilitation of these men should defame those who stayed in duty until the end of the war, if they did not commit any crime. It would be a success for the democratic state if one clearly and without doubt comes forward with the expectation that every single individual shall refuse to follow orders from an unjust regime. We did exactly that with the soldiers from the former East Germany. These soldiers were not punished or dishonoured here but were met with great understanding, welcomed in society and recognised as political refugees.

Not only the Central Council of Jews, the Green Party and the socialist party *Die Linke* ('The Left' or PDS, as they were then called) but also the German Evangelical Church synod demanded a revision of the Nazi sentences against those who had deserted from Hitler's *Wehrmacht* during the war. At its meeting at Borkum on 6 November 1996, the synod declared:

Some people are living among us who, between 1939 and 1945, were sentenced by the war tribunals for desertion, refusal to follow orders, and for *Wehrkraftzersetzung*. They are still seen as ex-convicts and this is no longer acceptable. The Second World War was a war of aggression and annihilation, a crime committed by the Nazis. The church at that time did not acknowledge this; today it must.

A person who refuses to participate in a crime deserves respect. To uphold sentences which have been passed against such a refusal is, when one looks at the criminal character of the Nazi dictatorship and its war, absurd. To withdraw oneself from such a crime can never be worthy of punishment. Rehabilitation of these deserters does not mean to belittle soldiers who believed they did their duty. They believed that they owed their Fatherland this, and they saw no way to withdraw. It is not about applying the same yardstick to all the armed forces. However, some units have, after orders from higher command, committed a severe injustice by shooting prisoners, carrying out massacres in occupied territories and assisting in the murder of Jews.

What a soldier does cannot be separated from his leaders' objective and moral sense. Love of one's Fatherland and courage can both be abused. They are only good virtues when they are used to pursue peace and procure freedom and justice. Rehabilitation of the victims cannot have a negative influence on the present defence forces. It is a democratic state. The constitution of the Federal State of Germany forbids any act in association with a war of aggression. Furthermore, soldiers are forbidden to follow a criminal order. The men and women who were once part of the opposition against the Nazi dictatorship today belong among the most essential role models for the present defence forces.

It was the Federal Supreme Social Court in Kassel (*Bundessozialgericht*) that first looked at this matter in a substantially different manner from earlier courts of justice.

In a sensational ruling of 1991, the judges declared that their colleagues in the Nazi military tribunals had been the extended arm of a criminal war campaign. They stated that the death sentences had been blatantly unjust and the military courts had willingly assisted the Nazi terror. Furthermore, it was declared that 'injustice has not only existed in problematic individual cases' and 'the war judges passed a large number of death sentences which do not meet the demands of a constitutional state'.

In order to substantiate their decision and illustrate what had influenced the war court lawyers, the Social Court judges cited the guiding phrase from the war years: 'The one who fears an honourable death dies in shame.' This view implied that he who refused the alleged honourable duty of a *Wehrmacht* soldier had lost the right to his life.

The background to this was a case in which the widow of an executed soldier had sued the state. Understandably – given the above statement – she won, was given compensation and granted a late war widow's pension. Knowing that there were many other women out there who now would come forward, the judges demanded that the law makers ensured that clear and unambiguous instructions were given for future cases.

Kassel's judges had sought support for their decision in facts disclosed by a self-taught amateur researcher. The name mentioned several times in the court ruling was Fritz Wüllner from Heidelberg. In 1987, together with Professor Manfred Messerschmidt, he had published a book, *Die Wehrmachtjustiz im Dienste des Nationalsozialismus. Zerstörung einer Legende.* (The War Courts in Service of National Socialism. Destruction of a Legend), that was to have huge importance.

Wüllner, after a career in insurance, retired early in order to find out the truth about what had happened to his brother Heinrich who had been killed during the war. His brother had participated in the attack on France in 1940, and the official version was that he had ended up in a penal battalion and had been shot during an attempt to escape. Wüllner did not believe that was the true story behind his brother's death and therefore dug deep into the war archives to find out what really happened. Unfortunately, the amateur researcher was unsuccessful, at least when it came to the original narrow project he had started off with. Wüllner found nothing about his brother Heinrich, but he did discover so much more. As he opened up the archives of the war courts, he was overwhelmed by the amount of information pointing at massive abuse and systematic terror, all unknown by post-war society. At this point it became clear for the first time how arbitrarily and ruthlessly the soldiers had been sentenced.

The earlier mentioned Hans Filbinger was one of many lawyers who turned up in these archives, but the name Erich Schwinge appeared much more often in the documents uncovered by Wüllner. It is therefore thanks to him that we today know about Schwinge's immense influence on Hitler's military justice, and that we have been made familiar with the previously mentioned barbaric death sentence against the boy Anton Reschny, who was reprieved at the last minute by Himmler.

The Kassel court declared that Nazi war justice could no longer be respected as legitimate. But this decision was not widely known publicly until the long-retired Professor Schwinge, then aged ninety, again returned to the limelight of publicity and vehemently aired his criticism. At the beginning of February 1993, he ranted and raged in the legal weekly *Neue Juristische Wochenschrift*: 'The supreme court in Kassel, with its U-turn, has with one stroke stigmatised thousands of people and suspected them of criminal activity.' As we will discover, Schwinge's compassion was not directed at the 20,000 victims of the Nazi executioners and judges. No, it was all about the lawyers' reputations. Schwinge was furious that these war judges, including himself, would suffer serious damage as a consequence of the Kassel verdict.

That this lawyer could continue his career and influence the system of justice right till the end of the 1980s can only be explained by the existing state of public repression. Very few had any desire to explore the old stories, and even fewer had the courage to challenge the old man's authority. For decades he belonged to a small group of lawyers who were seen as experts in this field and who could easily influence prevailing general and political opinion. The fact that Schwinge had passed his ninetieth birthday changed very little. For him it was business as usual, and he was listened to.

Schwinge propounded the thesis that the war judges had been in the service of the state and had therefore guaranteed individual legal rights also within the armed forces. Hence the Kassel verdict was a tremendous provocation for him. But it was a challenge for many others as well. After what had happened, the people of post-war Germany had a strong need to believe that at least the armed forces had been decent. Most individuals needed to believe this in order to come to terms with their nation's recent past, and the government was more than happy to join in the broadly accepted deception.

As late as 1986, one could read the following in a report to the parliament in Bonn:

> The sentences for refusal to do war service, desertion and *Wehrkraftzersetzung* have not breached the basic values of the constitutional state, as such legislation is an integral part of democratic states governed by law, and breaking of such laws is punishable in time of war.

Schwinge could have written that, but he had not, as there had been no need for him to do so. In 1986, and for many years to come, there was no shortage of people who could have written the same – and who did.

Chapter 23

A Tolerant Society

Incredible tolerance towards the perpetrators and callousness towards the victims was the order of the day. For Ludwig Baumann it was part of life, but he could never come to terms with it. On 3 March 1995, news about the issue again haunted him. On the radio it was reported that Wolfgang Lehnigk-Emden, a former *Wehrmacht* lieutenant who had been charged with war crimes and brought to trial, had been acquitted. 'In the name of the German people,' as it was stated, the Supreme Court had thrown out the case. The main reason behind the decision was that it was so long ago since the incidents had happened. Hence the now elderly Lehnigk-Emden not only remained free but was also to continue to be seen as a respectable law-abiding citizen. Fifteen women and children had been murdered, but, as the post-war delaying tactics had been so successful, 'it was now so long ago' – and why go for an old man?

Lehnigk-Emden had lived a peaceful life ever since this episode in Italy; he had swapped the brown for red and achieved prestigious positions as both carnival president and mayor of the town and, after he retired, he also had a legitimate claim to a pension covering his war duty. These were all reasons to feel disgust that this man had got off so easily. However, at the end of the day, the case against him was nothing more than just one example among thousands of others.

In the west, in the Federal Republic, a large number of Nazis and Nazi supporters regained their positions completely and were given a new chance; they were given Persil certificates and were allowed to start all over again as if nothing had happened. It applied at all levels, but one could say that the higher your status, the easier it was to be forgiven.

'What kind of a state is it that only absolves the murderers? What kind of state is it that today still claims that Hitler's judges in much of what they did were right? What kind of state is it that still punishes those who refused to take part in the murdering? I am almost in despair when I think of this state.'

Ludwig Baumann (more than half a century after he miraculously escaped Nazi war justice)

As many as twenty-one of these men ended up as either ministers or state secretaries in the Bonn administration, and around a hundred *Wehrmacht* officers continued their careers as generals and admirals in the *Bundeswehr*, as the armed forces had now, for whatever reason, been renamed. Further to that we can add 828 Nazi sympathisers and/or members of the Nazi party who continued to work as senior court officials, public prosecutors and judges in the judicial system; 245 men with dubious war backgrounds who ended up in leading positions in the German Foreign Office; and 297 senior Nazi officials who continued to serve in the post-war West German police force. We are here only talking about the very top. The real number of Nazis in the post-war West German administration was much larger than that.

However, as we have already seen, there was no point in a deserter applying for a job. The jobs were for the boys. While the 'traitors' were smeared, vilified and even beaten up, a former administrator of barbaric terror in the occupied east, Karl Friedrich Vialon, continued his career in Bonn. After a short stint as Chancellor Konrad Adenauer's adviser on economic and financial matters, Vialon became state secretary in the Ministry of Economic Co-operation. Vialon's list of sins is long, but the worst was his leading involvement in the so-called 'Final Solution' in the Baltic countries and Belarus. Among other duties, his role here was to strip Jewish victims of all their property before they were murdered by his colleagues who were trained for that purpose. With that kind of economic experience on his CV, this man continued his career after the war at the centre of West Germany's admired economic miracle.

While Vialon was busy with 'administration' in the east, one of his colleagues, Werner Best, made himself a name in occupied Denmark. But, as Best's records in Copenhagen cannot be described as flattering, the Danes showed little post-war gratitude for his services. He was held responsible for several murders in the country, among them the assassination of the national poet Kaj Munch. That could have meant the end of Best. Despite the death penalty in Denmark having been abolished in 1930, it was now, as the country was liberated, reintroduced and – quite extraordinarily and in itself not worthy of a constitutional state – made retroactive, i.e. made to apply to offences which had not been capital crimes at the time they were committed. Accordingly, after having been extradited from Germany, Best was sentenced to death. However, in stark contrast to condemned Danish traitors, the top-tier Nazi would get another chance, and a very favourable one. First, he had his sentence commuted to five years' imprisonment and, later, allegedly after a request from Bonn, he was pardoned and released. Best, not only the head administrator of the repression of Denmark and its people but also a convicted murderer, was needed at home; the Danes had to mete out justice on somebody else, somebody less important.

After returning home, Best was hired not only as a legal expert by the Hugo-Stinnes Group in Mülheim on the Ruhr but also by the West German Foreign Office. In 1972, new allegations were made against him, but though he would live for another seventeen years and spend lots of energy within the supportive network of old Nazis, he was now found medically unfit to stand trial – something we have heard of before when it comes to war criminals from the top echelon of society, not only in Germany.

Much of the information about Nazi war criminals and what happened to them after the war has been disclosed in recent years, but even in the 1960s most of it was available for anybody who wanted to know. As we have seen, the 'Brown Book' was published by the East German authorities. At the time, this detailed document was subject to massive western denunciation and accused of being nothing but a propaganda tool, but all these years later it is clear that the book told the truth. In fact, it is a surprisingly sober account; it does not just blame anybody. I am no defender of East German propaganda, but nowhere does the book come close to blaming all those millions of rank and file members of Nazi organisations who had been misled and duped. The people listed are those who held top positions in the Third Reich.

After realising how many they were, we also realise that there was little need for the German Democratic Republic (DDR) to look further down the ladder. That was done by western authorities, but only after all the real criminals were safely dead and beyond reach. First at this point the search for Nazi offenders started in a serious manner. Now, those who had been very young at the time of the war and who had served in low-key subordinate positions started to be held accountable for it all. John Demjanjuk is a good example of that.

After a long sequence of trials in Germany and Israel, Demjanjuk was finally charged with 27,900 counts of acting as an accessory to murder, one for each person who had died in Sobibór concentration camp at the time he was alleged to have served as a guard there. On 12 May 2011, he was sentenced to five years' imprisonment. Demjanjuk, who was ninety-one at the time Germany finally made him a scapegoat for its own war crimes, was born in Ukraine. He had been conscripted into the Red Army to fight Nazi aggression and was taken as a prisoner of war by German troops. Like all other private Soviet soldiers in Nazi war camps, he was subjected to freezing conditions and hunger. As the defence lawyer Ulrich Busch told the Munich court, sixty-five years later, even if Demjanjuk had, as claimed, chosen to volunteer as a prison guard, he had only done so because as a prisoner of war he would have either been shot by the Nazis or died of starvation.

I have no comment to make on whether Demjanjuk was a guard or not. My opinion is that it is disgusting to go after a conscripted foreigner like him, when all but a handful of the real war criminals were ever taken to court. As mentioned above, Werner Best was medically unfit to face justice, or so it was said, but ninety-year-old Demjanjuk was brought to the airport in an ambulance and flown to Germany to stand trial for 27,900 murders, though there was no evidence whatsoever that he had killed anybody.

There had been around 3,000 German war judges during the Second World War. After the capitulation many of these men continued to work in public office. Though some Nazi judges were tried at the Nuremberg Jurist Process, none of those cases were related to the military justice system. Only one of these lawyers, Rudolf Lehmann, was charged and sentenced in Nuremberg, but not for his war court activity. Lehmann had held two high legal positions during the war: he had been a colonel general staff judge, and leader of the *Wehrmacht*'s law department. In Nuremberg he was tried and sentenced for war crimes and crimes against humanity as part of the process against the highest command of the *Wehrmacht*. The seven years' imprisonment he was given was for his leading role in the Third Reich.

While Lehmann served a short stint behind bars, his colleagues from the military courts were left untouched. They went straight back to work, and shortly after the war had ended, they were heavily represented in almost all judicial authorities in the Federal Republic. Let us have a look at a few of them.

'The dagger of the assassin was concealed beneath the robe of the jurist.'

Prosecutor Telford Taylor at the Jurists' Trial in Nuremberg, 1947

Werner Hülle, who had been accused of deep involvement in Gen. Schörner's mass killing of war-weary German soldiers, and Otfried Keller, the expert we remember from the *Bundestag* hearing, both made it to become presidents of state courts, the former in Oldenburg and the latter in Marburg. But these are only two examples; there were many others. Former war judges were even active lawyers at the Nuremberg Jurist Process – as defence lawyers. They even built up their own unofficial union, the Association of Former Military Lawyers (*Verband ehemaliger Militärjuristen*). Having lost their political home, many found a replacement in the new Christian Union parties, the CDU and CSU.

In 1967, the CDU politician Gerhard Gaul became minister of justice in the state of Schleswig-Holstein and, in 1969, was appointed minister for trade and industry. From 1977 to 1979, Gaul served in a prominent position in the city administration of Lübeck, and at this time was honoured with the Federal *Bundesverdienstkreuz*, the Cross of Honour (equivalent to the UK honours). If we want to understand why specifically the conservative CDU and CSU for so many years and in such a passionate way protected the war criminals, Gaul is a good example. These people were friends, and, after the Nazis had changed political colour, they were also party colleagues. As senior judge in the navy, Gaul had been responsible for at least two death sentences during the war. The justification for one of these sentences was that 'asocial elements shall be eliminated without mercy'.

As we will notice again and again, Helmut Kohl's and Angela Merkel's CDU (Christian Democratic Union), founded in 1945, the year the Nazi party ceased to exist, absorbed many ex-Nazis with political ambitions. Gaul had been one, Filbinger another, but there were many more. Hans Krueger, another of Hitler's hanging judges, also changed from brown to black, the colour of the Christian party. He became a Member of Parliament in 1957 and continued to work as a lawyer as well. This man had joined the Nazi party in 1923, and following the attack on Poland had been appointed as special court judge in Konitz (Chojnice). Krueger was reputedly extremely brutal when passing sentences.

Other war judges who successfully continued their career in post-war West Germany are Matthias Hoogen, who had served Hitler in the Kurland Army and continued as commissioner for West Germany's Department of Defence, and Ernst Kanter, who had been chief war judge in Denmark. Kanter, a Nazi party member since 1933, had joined the war justice department in 1936 and had risen through the ranks with extraordinary speed. Just a year after he had been appointed, he was part of the inner circle of men responsible for the building up of the war court system needed for the planned aggression. When this work had been accomplished and the war started, Kanter began his active court career and was soon appointed as chief judge in occupied Denmark. Here there was a job to be done: the military leadership in Berlin had found military justice in Denmark too lax, but that opinion was based more on how the courts dealt with the locals than with how their own soldiers were treated. In spite of the Danish resistance fighters' ongoing acts of sabotage, at the time Kanter arrived no Danish civilians had been executed. That picture would now change. Shortly after Kanter had been installed, 103 Danes and twelve German soldiers were sentenced to death and shot.

After the war, this man was appointed president of the third criminal division of the supreme court in the Federal Republic. In this job, Kanter's responsibility was to investigate the wartime past of other still active Nazi lawyers within his geographical area, and so there is no reason to believe the old Nazi had changed sides. He was the same person he had always been and in no way tried to hide that. In the Düsseldorf edition of the newspaper *Deutsche Volkszeitung*, he wrote on 26 November 1957: 'It can be stated without more ado that disciplinary action for [having meted out] penal or disciplinary punishment cannot be justified.' With all his experience in dealing with suspect individuals, it was only logical that Judge Kanter would crown his successful career with a leading position in state security at the Federal Supreme Court. His duty there was to defend the state against domestic enemies.

Another man who had contributed profoundly to the creation of Nazi justice was lawyer Josef Schafheutle, and he was also recruited to the civil service in Bonn. Schafheutle became director at the Ministry of Justice. Commenting on his own achievements before and during the war, he said: 'The most important change was the toughening of penalties.'

Franz Schlegelberger was acting minister of justice in 1941-42. The notorious 'undercover decree', which provided for the imprisonment of all Hitler opponents without an arrest warrant, was his work. Of course, it would be impossible to mention all the criminal activity that took place in this department during Schlegelberger's time in office, but one other decree might also be worth mentioning. This decree, directed against a specific nationality – the Poles – instructed all special courts to pass death sentences for the slightest offence committed by any of these people. At Nuremberg, Schlegelberger was sentenced to life imprisonment, but his stay behind bars cannot have lasted that long, as in the 1960s he was given a generous pension from Bonn for his service to the state. His son Hartwig had followed in his father's footsteps and had been even luckier; he was never held to account. After serving Hitler as a senior staff judge in the navy, he pursued a post-war career as home minister of Schleswig-Holstein.

In fact, these people were everywhere. Let us mention just a few more examples. Leonhard Drach was promoted as public prosecutor in Frankenthal in 1956. During the war, he had served as prosecutor at courts martial and special courts in occupied Luxemburg. In that position, Drach had successfully called for many death sentences. After the war, a Luxemburg court sentenced him for war crimes, but, as was always the case, he was soon out of jail and back in office.

Rudolf Albrecht, who had belonged to the 17th Army as a senior war court judge, chose to work as a post-war lawyer in Munich. His colleague Rudolf Aichinger continued as a solicitor in Weissenburg, and Heinrich Arnold, who had served as an army judge in France, did the same but in Memmingen. Army judge Erich Barbier from the 46th Infantry Division used his experience in a post-war career as director of a local court in Frankenthal. Eberhard Baring, senior military judge, became president of the Social Court in Celle. Rudolf Becker, senior military court counsellor in the *Wehrmacht* headquarters in Berlin, continued after the war as court director in Dortmund. Ludwig Fink, military court counsellor of the 407th Infantry Division, became public prosecutor in Kempten. Gustav Kress, military court counsellor in the 413th Infantry Division, became senior judge in Schwabach. Konrad Lenski, military court counsellor in both the Supreme Military Court in Torgau and the 6th Field Military Court, continued after the war as court director in Lüneburg. Ulrich Schattenberg, chief court counsellor in the navy, ended up as public prosecutor in Lübeck, though he, like all the others, rightfully should have found himself in the dock. I will not mention them all here, but the list goes on and on.

Though these people were never expected to risk their own life and limb, they happily passed sentences on 'cowards' and war resisters in the name of Hitler, and, after the war, they continued to tell others what was wrong and what was right – now in the name of Adenauer.

In fact, it is interesting that they were allowed back. After all, the Allied Control Council had decreed in Article IV of its law No. 4 of 30 October 1945, based on the Potsdam Agreement:

> For the purpose of transforming the German legal system [back to a state of democratic constitutional law], all previous members of the Nazi party who took an active part in its activities and all other persons who were directly involved in Nazi methods of punishment must be removed from their positions as judges and public prosecutors and may not be re-admitted to such offices.

Moreover, it would have been the same men the international judges had in mind when, during the Nuremberg Jurists Trials, they came to the very important conclusion that not only had the draconic Nazi legal organisation in itself constituted a crime against humanity but that all the Nazi laws, decrees and regulations that its officials had used as legal support for their criminal activity did as well. It was also a violation of the Hague Agreement on Land Warfare when special courts were set up in countries invaded by foreign troops, in this case the *Wehrmacht*. As Hitler's military courts also assumed the role of special courts for the civilian population in some occupied states like Holland, Belgium, France, Norway and Denmark, that was in clear violation of international law as well. The individual lawyers were personally responsible for all that.

However, not only did they get away with it but everything was done to make their retirement comfortable. The pensions given to these people were legally fixed by paragraph 116 of the West German Judges' Law, passed by parliament on 8 September 1961 in the wake of the East German disclosure of these Nazis' continued careers in the west. West Germany was now eager to remove the Nazis from sight and encouraged them to give up work. In accordance with this legislation, those hanging judges who agreed to retire would receive full pensions even before reaching retirement age. In this way, a large number of these men with blood-soaked hands disappeared from public office in the early 1960s. They were all rewarded with generous pensions for their loyal service to their Fatherland.

Much of the early attention on the continuing careers of these men had been due to revelations by Communists in East Berlin. But, as we will see, the German Democratic Republic had its own skeletons in the cupboard, though far fewer. Not even there, in the sworn anti-Fascist state, were Nazis completely excluded from continuing their careers, even in very high office. Some – the most adaptable turncoats – managed pretty well.

Chapter 24

The Browns Change Colour

Not despite his past as a war judge but more likely because of the qualifications and experiences he had earned as such, Kurt Schumann was reinstated as a lawyer very soon after he had started a new life in the newly founded German Democratic Republic (DDR). The young state needed his expertise, and, as he was well qualified and in desperate need of a fresh start, the comrades knew they could count on his political loyalty.

Schumann had not only been a proficient war judge and loyal member of the Nazi party but also turned out to be a master political turncoat and opportunist as well. After having been captured by the Red Army at the end of the war, he quickly joined the National Committee for a Free Germany (*Das Nationalkomitee Freies Deutschland*) and declared himself 'reformed'. He was forgiven for his Nazi past and swapped sides. Schumann was now a Communist, and as such he would come to serve as East Germany's highest judge – as president of the Supreme Court in East Berlin. In this new role, the former Nazi would for the next eleven years loyally guard the Communist constitution and agenda.

However, everything comes to an end; in 1960, he was forced to leave. Had the Communists finally come to the conclusion that a Nazi as their supreme judge might be a bit dodgy? No; the reason Schumann had to resign was due to the new blame game between the two post-war German states. As the East Germans had started their discrediting campaign about all the old Nazis working for the West German authorities, it appeared they had shot themselves in the foot. Bonn started a counter-campaign, and that is what suddenly made Schumann a liability. He became a burden to the party and had to be removed. Trial and jail? No; he was given a job as law professor at the renowned Humboldt University, a post he kept until he retired in 1973.

Another example of Nazis in East Germany was Arno von Lenski. Despite a past as a Nazi party member and regardless of a successful career as both a People's Court expert and a senior *Wehrmacht* officer, he made it to the top of East Germany's state administration. Von Lenski was a descendant of an old aristocratic family, but he was also successful in his own right. In 1938, he had reached the rank of colonel, and soon after the outbreak of war he was promoted to lieutenant general and appointed as commander of the 24th Armoured Division. But that was not enough for a man with high aspirations. He was a man with special talents, and (along with his military career) this had led to him being recruited to the People's Courts – by Hitler himself. Here he would serve as a military expert and adviser and was assigned to the third criminal division of the court system, which specialised in treason, defeatism, draft avoidance and, of course, *Wehrkraftzersetzung*.

However, von Lenski's busy Nazi career also came to an abrupt halt. In 1943, he was taken prisoner by the Soviets after his armoured division had been almost completely wiped out at the Battle of Stalingrad, and this was the first step in a radical political transformation. Von Lenski decided to swap sides, and, as a first step, he became a member of the National Committee for a Free Germany. This led him to be sentenced to death in absentia by the war courts in Torgau, but he was well beyond their reach.

In 1949, von Lenski returned to Germany, to the new Communist DDR, and was accepted as a victim of the Nazi regime. Having achieved that, his new life began. The Nazi was now a convinced and devoted Communist, and he started to ascend another career ladder. After first having served in the police force and thereafter at the home office, he was appointed ministerial leader of East Germany's armoured contingents in 1956, was elected member of the East German parliament and was nominated to the boards of both the national Olympic Committee and the DDR-Soviet Friendship Organisation.

But, unfortunately for von Lenski, then came the above-mentioned inter-German smear campaigns, and, as had happened to Schumann, von Lenski would also end up in Bonn's searchlight. To counter the accusations about all its own Nazis in top positions, West Germany started to show great interest in von Lenski's new life, and consequently his second career also neared its end. The DDR leaders, now under pressure, had to ask him to go. He did, but he would not want for anything. Retiring with the rank of a DDR army general, he was given a pension that also would cover the years he had spent in the *Wehrmacht*. In no way could the disclosure of von Lenski's past have come as a surprise to the East German leadership, as he had never tried to hide it. Already at the end of the war, he had disclosed all about his background to officials of the Communist Party – among them Walter Ulbricht.

Von Lenski must have had a talent for making new friends, all of whom seemed to hold him in high esteem, no matter where he was. As a consequence, he received numerous military and political honours from both sides of the Communist/Fascist divide. Among them were the Bavarian Military Merit Order, Austria's (!) Military Merit Cross, the German Cross in Gold, the East German Patriotic Order of Merit in Gold, and (awarded by East Germany to an ex-Nazi party member, kangaroo-court expert and Hitlerite officer …) the Medal for Fighters Against Fascism.

Responsible Production

Arms manufacturers like Krupp, Stinnes, Röchling, Kirdorf and Thyssen made themselves huge fortunes during the First World War, all with weapons that caused enormous suffering and even gave medicine a new diagnosis. The horror their newly invented terror weapons caused was the reason behind Harry Farr's affliction; because of Krupp and his colleagues, Harry came to suffer from shell shock; because of them he ended up being shot by his own comrades.

Yet, for industrialists producing weapons, the First World War was a big smorgasbord. The German state financed the conversion and adaptation of its industries from civilian to military production; the factories were offered secure long-term contracts, and they were paid more or less what they asked for. That Harry and all his proletarian colleagues on both sides of the trenches had no personal interest in the fighting except to stay alive; that these young men's lives, whether they survived or not, were destroyed in the madness of total destruction; that their limbs would not stop shaking; that they were shot at dawn if they could no longer cope; none of that mattered. It was a war about power and influence; it was about commodities, business and commerce, and in order to keep the common people on all sides loyal to the great cause, it was all sold as 'defence of the Fatherland'.

The Kaiser and Krupp walked hand in hand, were even family friends, and, as Rosa Luxemburg bitterly stated: 'The dividends rise and the proletarians fall.' What she did not know at the time was that this was just the beginning of really good business. However, she did know that the war could only be stopped if the soldiers refused to co-operate in their own destruction. Rosa Luxemburg left the Social Democratic Party after they had chosen to support the war, and she helped form the *Internationale* group of revolutionaries. She and her co-campaigners wanted German soldiers to desert and turn their weapons against their own oppressors.

The arms industry had had a golden age during the Great War, and more good times would come with the build-up to the Second World War. Again the industrialists would benefit and the ordinary soldiers from humble backgrounds would die miserable deaths, either on the battlefields or in front of the firing squads. So what happened to these dealers in death when it was all over? Were they deprived of power and fortunes and properly punished? Were they made responsible? Not really, but initially it looked like something would happen. In three separate trials after the war, German industrialists were tried by US military courts for war crimes. Krupp, IG Farben and Flick were the companies in question.

These firms had not only produced much of the weaponry used by the *Wehrmacht* but had also been deeply involved in a range of Nazi activities; they had facilitated most of the killings, not just what took place on the battlefields. In IG Farben's case, the most difficult thing to explain was that of Zyklon B, the poison gas supplied to the death camps. But, for all these industrialists, not only the chemists, the charges were extremely serious: the term 'war crime' covers them all.

We will be surprised when we look at the sentences. Of the twenty-four defendants in the IG Farben trial, thirteen were found guilty and sentenced to prison terms ranging from one-and-a-half to eight years. Despite the extensive evidence presented by the prosecution, which showed that the company had been deeply involved in Germany's re-armament after the First World War, the tribunal did not find them guilty of having helped prepare a war of aggression. Even when it came to the charges of having used slave labour, the judges allowed the accused to use the defence that it had been a 'necessity'. Only in the case of Auschwitz, where IG Farben had constructed a plant next to the extermination camp with the clear intent to use inmates as slave workers, did the tribunal consider the evidence sufficient to prove that the company had acted on its own initiative. For this, the chairman of the board, Carl Krauch, was sentenced to six years' imprisonment.

A slightly more severe sentence was handed out to another member of the board, Fritz ter Meer. He had been in charge of IG Farben's chemical plant near Auschwitz and had also been planning a satellite camp to the infamous extermination site. When this man was interviewed in Nuremberg regarding his view on tests on humans in Auschwitz, he replied that the question was irrelevant: 'They were prisoners, thus no particular harm was inflicted, as they would have been killed anyway.' In 1948, Fritz ter Meer was sentenced to seven years in prison, but, along with the others sentenced with him, he was released in 1950 for 'good behaviour'. Thereafter he continued as supervisory board chairman of Bayer AG, a chemical firm best known for its role in the invention of aspirin. For a number of years, until IG Farben was dissolved after the war due to the war crimes, Bayer AG had been a part of that chemical conglomerate.

In the case of Flick, Friedrich Flick himself and five other directors were in the dock. Friedrich Flick was also charged with war crimes and crimes against humanity. The firm had participated in the deportation and enslavement of civilian populations in other countries and territories; they had used slaves in their mines and factories and confiscated industries in France, Poland and Russia. Flick himself got seven years, two of his co-defendants shorter sentences, and the three others were acquitted.

At the Krupp trial, twelve former directors of the Krupp Group were accused of having enabled the armament of German military forces and thus actively participated in the preparations for an aggressive war. The charges were: (a) crimes against peace by participating in the planning and waging of wars of aggression and wars in violation of international treaties; (b) crimes against humanity by participating in the plundering, devastation and exploitation of occupied countries; (c) crimes against humanity by participating in the murder, extermination, enslavement, deportation, imprisonment and torture of civilians and prisoners of war; and (d) participating in a conspiracy to commit crimes against peace.

The main defendant, Alfried Krupp von Bohlen und Halbach, was sentenced to twelve years and was ordered to sell all his possessions. The others got lesser sentences and one defendant was acquitted. On 31 January 1951, two and a half years after having been charged and sentenced, all but one were released from prison. And since no buyer for the Krupp company had been found, Alfried Krupp resumed control in 1953. In 1968, it became a corporation and, in 1999, the Krupp Group merged with its largest competitor Thyssen AG (in existence since before the First World War). The largest shareholder of

ThyssenKrupp AG today is the Alfried Krupp von Bohlen and Halbach Foundation, a major German philanthropic foundation, created by and named in honour of the former head of the organisation.

Military men in the *Bundeswehr*

While Ludwig Baumann, haunted by his war experiences, looked for comfort in the bottle and was left to make a meagre income as a door-to-door salesman of curtains, the producers of the weaponry that had killed and maimed so many were preparing for a comfortable life in post-war society. And the same was the case for those who had given the orders on or behind the battlefields.

As early as 1950, re-militarisation of West Germany was on the political agenda, and despite conscripted German armies already twice in the previous thirty-six years having been the prime reason for worldwide destruction and mass killing, young German men were again to be forced into military service. The Allies allowed it; after all, other German young men had already been lined up on the other side of the iron curtain as their new enemies. Another important reason was that Adenauer's government aspired to NATO membership, and unemployed Hitlerite officers were waiting for their chance to get back to work. So the stage was set for another major professional comeback, and, in 1955, after ten years out in the cold, these men returned to the barracks.

As a *Wehrmacht* officer, Heinz Trettner had quickly worked himself up the ranks and was highly respected, not least for his contribution to the planning of the invasion of the Netherlands. He had lived up to what was expected of him, and we know what the army saw as essential virtues. Even better, Trettner had stayed loyal to the very end of the war and had been generously decorated for his patriotism.

After a brief spell in American captivity and after having updated himself in economics and law (obviously not enough to realise his own culpability), this airman parachuted himself right back into what was now the *Bundeswehr*, the renamed armed forces of the new Federal state. Göring's air force, the Luftwaffe, was no more, but one of its officers – a man who had thought it acceptable to attack peaceful neighbours in Hitler's name – was reinstated in its successor institution and enabled to continue his military career, first as major general and head of logistics at the NATO headquarters in Paris and then, as a final achievement, as inspector general of West Germany's entire armed forces. These military forces had now been given other names, but many of those pulling the strings in the *Bundeswehr* were the same as before. Trettner was just one of them, though he had reached the top.

Let us name a few others who were also successful in their new lives. Gen. Johann Adolf von Kielmansegg had been a Nazi of the worst sort. But, even so, that was no problem. At a time when deserters were vilified, smeared and banned from simple jobs, this officer climbed back onto the career ladder and became head of NATO's land forces in central Europe. Von Kielmansegg had written extensively about his own Fascist convictions, so we know well where he stood on certain issues:

We are happy to report that we have completed the task that history, Germany and the Führer have asked us to fulfil, and we are happy to report that we are now prepared to exterminate England in the same way, the country that alone stands between us and freedom.

When this man wrote about bombing and devastation, he used such phrases as 'This tremendous, overwhelming scene lasted for four hours; a wonderful picture unfolded before our very eyes,' and 'The tanks crush all resistance in their path.' After the war he was one of Adenauer's chief military advisers.

Lt Adolf Heusinger loyally served the Kaiser during the First World War. During the inter-war Weimar Republic, Capt. Heusinger was a patriotic officer in the *Reichswehr* and, after Hitler had come to power, he reached the top and acted briefly as Chief of the General Staff of the *Wehrmacht*. As had happened at the end of the Great War, after the Second World War the brave warrior spent time in British/western captivity, but as soon as that was over he was again ready for promotion. From 1957 to 1961, Inspector General Heusinger served as head of West Germany's *Bundeswehr*, and thereafter reached even higher and became chairman of NATO's Military Committee in Washington. When the successful soldier later retired from active duty, he was hired as a military adviser to the governing CDU/CSU parties back in Bonn. It has been reported that he was wanted by the Soviets at that time, suspected of having organised a massacre while in charge of troops invading the country.

Karl-Adolf Zenker, after working his way up through the naval hierarchy, was transferred to the operational department of the navy's supreme command. In spirit, Zenker was a Fascist officer who adored Raeder and Dönitz, and while serving them he learned his craft. With the rebuilding of the navy from 1951, these experiences would be put to good use. From then on, Zenker served his country as a naval expert and adviser. But it was obvious that not much had changed in the head of this old Nazi. At an oath of allegiance ceremony for new recruits on 16 January 1956 in Wilhelmshaven, he said that every old navy man (he meant himself and his wartime colleagues) knows that the careers of the two former commanders-in-chief of the navy (Raeder and Dönitz) had been spotless and beyond reproach. Eleven years after the war, Capt. (later Vice Adml) Zenker told the new seamen of the reborn navy that the only question for him and his colleagues had been whether it was appropriate for them to go back to duty whilst their former commanders still were in jail:

Only from the honourable German point of view that it was a strictly necessary duty for us to defend our common liberty, it could be regarded as justified to disregard our old comrades' fates in such a manner.

In his book *Als Jagdflieger in Spanien* (As a Fighter Pilot in Spain), published in 1936, Johannes Trautloft told his own early story in detail. After having been sent to Spain in order to help General Franco's rebels, Lt Trautloft's belligerent ambitions were satisfied for the first time. From these days of the Spanish Civil War, he wrote:

We are allowed to fight, and that satisfies us completely. It seems like our primitive instincts have been suppressed, but now the instincts of the hunter are breaking through again. We have found the way back to the beginning of mankind, and that will ensure that the age of our white race will last for another long time. How philistine it is, when people claim we have reverted to barbarism.

Describing how he and his friends had attacked the little village of Santa Olalla in Toledo province, he boasts:

While flying low, we fired our machine-gun volleys at the enemy; I saw a lorry, which suddenly had been deprived of its driver, swerve sideways and turn over. Human beings crept forth from the rubbish, many staggered, fell and lay still. Certainly, nothing can satisfy a soldier more than the sight of his confused, panic-stricken enemy desperately trying to escape.

In another murderous attack in which he took part, sixty-three children and numerous adults were killed in Getafe, a suburb of Madrid. The children were crushed by the rubble as their school was bombed, according to Trautloft. However, a newspaper account from the following day states that they were blown to pieces by bombs dropped on them while playing in the street. No matter how they died, the crime is known as the 'massacre of the children of Getafe'. This was Trautloft's view on the matter: 'The work accomplished today is extraordinary.' After 1945, Trautloft was allowed to devote himself to helping rebuild the *Bundeswehr*. He retired with the rank of lieutenant general in 1970.

Let us look at one final example. Hans Speidel's CV from the war would hardly qualify him for a peace prize. But this *Wehrmacht* major general, like so many of his colleagues, went on to enjoy a successful post-war career. First he became a professor of modern history, a history he had helped so much to make, and thereafter he joined the *Bundeswehr*, attained the rank of full general, and, as the icing on the cake, was appointed NATO's commander-in-chief of ground forces in Europe. Between 1957 and 1963, he was the highest ranking military man in western Europe.

Chapter 25

Struggle for Rehabilitation

It had taken time, but the 1991 ruling of the Federal Supreme Social Court in favour of a widow of a deserter, thanks to the research by Fritz Wüllner and Manfred Messerschmidt, slowly opened a door. From then on, the political establishment was put under pressure not only by the new Federal Union of Victims of Nazi Military Justice, chaired by Ludwig Baumann, but also by a new generation of lawyers.

In 1995, it was declared by the Supreme Court that the war courts had deliberately perverted and illegitimately used the concept of justice and had therefore committed a crime. The Nazi judges' successors in the highest court of the country even declared that their retired colleagues had been 'blood judges'. Though this clear-cut ruling did not lead to legal action against any individual judge, it did help push the politicians into some sort of action. On 15 May 1997, most probably due to all the years of lobbying, something happened. An official declaration was issued from Bonn that was to constitute a breakthrough in the campaign for justice. 'The Second World War was an act of aggression and annihilation, a criminal act committed by Nazi Germany,' it said.

This was definitely a step forward, but despite the state now openly declaring what the whole world had already known for half a century, it was still far from satisfactory. There was a snag attached to the new position: the declaration maintained that the sentences passed on deserters had been unjust only if 'their acts today would not constitute a crime'. As desertion is still a criminal offence and offenders are liable to prosecution, not much had changed. Consequently, after the declaration had been followed by a law on 25 August 1998, *Gesetz zur Aufhebung der NS-Unrechtsurteile* (an Act repealing unjust Nazi sentences), the deserters from Hitler's forces were still not rehabilitated. The men who had been sentenced for war refusal, *Wehrkraftzersetzung*, treason (but not military treason), a failure of duty in the field, surrender to the enemy and espionage had their sentences annulled and were rehabilitated, but the deserters and war traitors were not.

This was, of course, a major disappointment. The deserters' association had struggled for a long time; they had been firm in their insistence that the sentences should be annulled without any preconditions, but that had not happened. The text only said that a deserter or other victim of military justice could have his individual case heard. Only by proving that he as an individual had not committed a criminal offence could he achieve personal rehabilitation. It was clearly stated and repeatedly emphasised that a blanket rehabilitation of all those sentenced by the war courts was out of the question. The most likely reason for that position was the repeatedly used excuse that such rehabilitation of war resisters would automatically stigmatise all those who had remained loyal and continued to serve. That proponents of a blanket rehabilitation throughout the years had again and again refuted that claim had not made much of a difference.

As chair of the victims' association, Ludwig declared:

> The old men who are still alive shall not have to go to the public prosecutor; we shall not let them put us through such a disgraceful procedure. These men shall not walk this humiliating path.

For Ludwig, nothing was acceptable except unconditional rehabilitation for both those still alive and those who had died.

The struggle continued, now with the help of the socialist party *Die Linke*. With their help things gradually changed, and on 17 May 2002, shortly before the end of that sitting of parliament, another milestone was reached when a bill introduced by the small left-wing party passed into law. A small majority, consisting of social democrats, greens and members of *Die Linke*, had outweighed the only slightly fewer opponents on the right of the political spectrum and had finally rehabilitated the deserters.

Legally, most of Hitler's defiant soldiers were now rehabilitated and were no longer to be considered as ex-convicts with a criminal record. But, as we have seen, only slightly more than half of the nation's political representatives had voted in favour of this law – far from the overwhelming enthusiastic majority that would have been needed to draw a proper line between past and present. And, importantly, four categories of sentenced soldiers had been removed from the final text of the law, among them war traitors. It can be concluded that, fifty-seven years after the end of the war, more than half of the political representatives of the German people still recognised sentences passed by Hitler's military courts; in 2002, more than half of the *Bundestag* still recognised those courts as legitimate legal institutions.

These remaining difficulties in coming to terms with this issue can be explained, if not defended. The collective guilt was tremendous. In order to live, people need to repress mentally what cannot be properly dealt with, and in post-war Germany this repression existed across the nation. Consequently there was a tendency to distinguish between the Fatherland and the Nazi movement, and there was an attempt to portray the Second World War as two different wars: the fight for the Fatherland on the one hand, and the fight for the Nazi party on the other. The armed forces, the *Wehrmacht*, were seen more as part of the Fatherland than of the ruling Nazi party; hence, the deserter had let down his Fatherland and not opposed the Nazis. The fact that those three concepts – the Fatherland, the Nazis and the *Wehrmacht* – had been closely entwined for many years before and during the war was conveniently forgotten. For the majority of the population, that was the easiest way out of a conundrum.

However, in this context it is important to stress that millions of German soldiers had to fight in that war and millions of them died on the battlefields after unimaginable suffering. Others survived but were devastated mentally and physically. No one, including the author of this book, has the right to pass judgement on the extent to which the individual who stayed loyal acted out of personal pro-Nazi conviction, a sense of duty toward the Fatherland, or out of sheer fear. We have no right to judge those who succumbed to military coercion when the only alternative was certain death. But that same right not to be judged should also apply to those who, for whatever reason, refused to follow orders and withdrew from duty in a criminal regime's armed forces.

A memorable day

An elderly gentleman in a red anorak sat unnoticed in the courtyard of Bendlerblock, Berlin. During the Second World War, the Supreme Command of the Armed Forces, the *Wehrmacht*, had used these buildings, and it was here, fifty-six years earlier, that Claus Schenk Graf von Stauffenberg and four other officers, members of the conspiracy of 20 July, were executed in the eerie beams of a lorry's headlights.

Every year since 1952, on the anniversary of this event, the German government remembers and honours these murdered resisters, the heroes who attempted to put a full stop to Hitler and the Nazis' reign of violence and terror. They are said to be heroes of democracy, even though many of them would rather have seen a strong, authoritarian Germany than the establishment of a true and peaceful democracy.

The Federal armed forces of Germany, the *Bundeswehr*, under Minister of Defence Rudolph Scharping were the hosts for this celebration, and widows of some of the executed were guests of honour. *'Ich hatt' einen Kameraden'* ('I Had a Comrade') and the national anthem were played, and there were many speakers, the most prominent of whom was the Speaker of the *Bundestag*, Wolfgang Thierse. The speakers talked about 'resistance [against evil]' and claimed it was 'fundamental for our republic'. They also stressed that 'the conspirators had followed their conscience and morality'. Beautiful words, and many people were moved.

In one way, this particular evening differed from all the previous ones, even if this slight variation passed unnoticed by the majority of those present. For the first time ever, the memory of the imprisoned and executed conscientious objectors and deserters was also to be honoured. One of them, one of the few who were still alive, was wearing a red anorak this evening, and he was to lay a wreath. Ludwig Baumann was happy to have that honour. But, the hope he had also cherished was not to be fulfilled. None of the speakers mentioned the group to which he had belonged, so many of whom had been murdered. True, Thierse spoke about the importance of a broad understanding of the word 'resistance': 'Resistance starts with the small acts, with the secretly smuggled piece of bread to the forced labourer and stretches to the murder attempt against the inhuman dictator,' he said, before going on to encourage the struggle against ultra-right extremism in society. 'Never more must a silent majority not feel a sense of responsibility when basic human rights are infringed.' When he had finished speaking, and accompanied by drum-rolls and soldiers presenting arms, he laid a wreath in honour of the murdered officers.

Ludwig himself was not a guest of honour. He was not even officially invited, and was not mentioned in any of the speeches. Permission had been given for the laying of a wreath, but this and the speech Ludwig would give could only take place after the official part, the 'proper' part, of the memorial ceremony had ended. The guests had begun to leave the courtyard as the deserter and his friends walked forward, and only one of the VIP guests remained, the Bishop of the Evangelical Church in Berlin-Brandenburg, Wolfgang Huber. However, this did not prevent Ludwig from knowing that with his wreath he was remembering 20,000 murdered soldiers, most of them simple men who had been executed for their own act of resistance. Ludwig did not lay it beside the memorial tablet for these officers who for years had loyally served Hitler and changed sides only when they no longer saw the chance of winning the war. He put it at the feet of a statue of a naked young man with his hands tied.

After that wreath had also been laid and the peace activists were about to leave, a distasteful episode happened – Ludwig was suddenly verbally attacked and accused of being a blatant criminal by the commander of the memorial security staff. But at least he had been officially 'tolerated' by the defence forces, and it had been a significant and memorable day.

> 'What could you have done better than betray Hitler's war?'
>
> *Ludwig Baumann*

With its memorial tablet for the 20 July conspiracy and Professor Richard Scheibes' statue of a young naked man with his hands tied, the Court of Honour is the central point of Bendlerblock in Berlin, now a resistance museum. It was beside this statue that Ludwig Baumann laid his wreath.

On the same day, at another gathering, Minister of Defence Scharping said in a speech that 20 July 1944 was a symbol of the resistance against the Nazi regime; that 'within the armed forces, soldiers had known the meaning of serving an unjust regime and had listened to their conscience and risked their lives'. These words referred to the executed officers, but were more apposite to the people represented by Ludwig. Unfortunately, that was not the intended meaning. Next morning, the wreath at the feet of the young man with his hands tied had been removed.

Two years later, Ludwig and other members of the peace movement again attempted to lay a wreath in connection with the official memorial celebration at Bendlerblock. However, this time nothing came of their plans. The government and the *Bundeswehr* had decided to have a 'closed event' or, as they also expressed it, a 'trouble-free' one. It seemed that the mere presence of a Second World War deserter and a few anti-war activists was seen as 'trouble'.

Chapter 26

A New Era in Torgau

As late as 2001, it was no surprise for Ludwig Baumann to be treated as a pariah in a situation like the one just described. He was used to it; after all, in West Germany where he lived, it had been like that for over half a century: a Hitler deserter was not a welcome guest when it came to patriotic events. However, in the other Germany, the German Democratic Republic, the part ruled firstly by a Soviet military administration and then, after 1949, by the Socialist Unity Party (*Die Sozialistische Einheitspartei Deutschlands*), the Communist SED, it had not been much better. Not even there, in the anti-Fascist workers' paradise, had Nazi war resisters been seen as role models unless, of course, they had been Communists. There had been an obvious reason for that: concepts like desertion and refusal to follow orders did not fit easily into the glorious picture of accepted behaviour in the young socialist dictatorship. For the new ruling class it was important that young people were not given too many ideas.

Of those victims of Nazi crimes who came to live in East Germany, only a few were recognised as such by the young socialist state. In fact, being a victim was not enough – one had to be the right sort of victim, a Communist, and the persecution must have been related to that political conviction. Even that was not sufficient to be formally classified as a proper victim of Hitler's terror regime. The hopeful applicant also had to prove that he or she had served a minimum of eighteen months in jail. That condition would have been almost impossible to meet for a former *Wehrmacht* soldier who had been sentenced by a Hitler war court. After all, a penal battalion did not count as a prison. Owing to these obstacles, most of these men remained unrecognised and disrespected for whatever they had done or not done during the war.

This was so, even though a large number of old Nazis, including many war judges, had been sentenced for war crimes as part of the Waldheim Trials, the legal processes against Nazis held after the war in the small East German town of Waldheim. Unlike in the west, in the Communist DDR Nazi officials and other war criminals were charged and many were sentenced. In addition to approximately 3,000 prison sentences, thirty-two death sentences were passed, and of these the largest part were against serious war criminals, among them war judges.

At least ten military court lawyers were tried and sentenced in Waldheim. Here it is important to remember that they were sentenced for their roles as judges and prosecutors – for having been part of the judicial killing of German soldiers. Six of those judges were sentenced to death, and four of them – Alfred Herzog, Walter Karl Schmidt, Horst

Rechenbach and Johannes Hommel – were executed. Johannes Müller and Werner Zieger had their sentences commuted to life in prison. Nevertheless, contrary to what one might have expected, even in the east and despite the Waldheim Trials, the Nazi war courts and the injustice they had committed were by and large regarded as taboo and off-limits for any serious discussion.

After the war, detentions in Torgau continued. The former military prisons were still used, but now by other rulers. From 1945 to 1950, the Soviet military administration used these buildings as central camps, and between 1950 and 1989 they served East Germany as prisons. This is where we again meet the judges, now on the other side of the bars. According to official Soviet Union statistics, of the 7,672 prisoners who were held in Fort Zinna in January 1946, 5,406 had been active members of the Nazi party. More specifically, out of these Nazis, 498 had been members of the Gestapo or the SD and 102 men had held leading positions in different concentration camps.

However, the Waldheim Trials were themselves problematic. First, it can be argued that, as with the Nazi mock courts, they had not provided anything like fair trials; and, second, political opponents of the Communist regime had also been tried and punished as part of these processes. Many years later these facts would lead to a bitter and painful conflict of interests.

The period after the 1990 collapse of East Germany and the merger of east and west into a new Federal Republic was a time of great urgency. There was a longing for immediate change and political reform, at least in so far as it concerned the forty years of Communist rule in the eastern part of the country. One thing that was rushed through at the earliest opportunity was the SED Injustice Law, and the Waldheim Trials became part of this new legislation. As these processes were now seen as nothing but Communist persecution of the opposition, all the sentences they had passed were with a stroke of a pen declared null and void. All defendants in these trials forty years earlier were presented with blanket rehabilitation.

However, what at the time was seen as a fair response to a former dictatorship and its now defunct prejudiced court system would soon turn out to be just a further example of gross injustice. With the blanket rehabilitation not only were the political opponents who had been sentenced in Waldheim declared innocent victims of persecution – something that was perfectly correct and beyond reproach – but the same was automatically the case with all Nazi criminals who had been sentenced along with them. All these men were also declared innocent, wrongly sentenced and fully rehabilitated, and were awarded damages. They were now to be seen as victims of a dictatorial regime. As we will see, this blanket rehabilitation of war criminals would cause long-term distress to the few surviving victims of Hitler's war courts. Whether on purpose or due to unbelievable incompetence, the legislators had passed a law that was controversial to say the least.

When, in 1992, a three-metre high cross was unveiled in front of the infamous prison of Fort Zinna in Torgau, a bitter and painful struggle started. The cross had been an attempt to commemorate all victims of the two recent dictatorships ruling Torgau. But, as will become clear, the implication of this merger of different groups into one monument was serious. With this cross all victims suffering under Hitler – Jews, Roma and others – would be remembered by a monument that also celebrated the memory of condemned war criminals.

Responsibility for the policy on memorials in the state of Saxony lay with the Foundation of Saxony Memorials and, unfortunately, it was soon clear that this had not been a tragic mistake by them. It had been intentional. For the Foundation – and this has been confirmed on numerous occasions since – the victims from after 1945 were (and are) far more important than the victims of the Nazi terror regime. The victims of East Germany came first, the victims of Hitler second. And that war criminals were included in the memorial was flatly denied. It was claimed that the cross was dedicated to the 'unrightfully persecuted' victims, and that those who had committed crimes were therefore not included. However, nothing could be more wrong. As those men who had been sentenced in Waldheim for Nazi crimes had been rehabilitated, they were from a legal point of view innocent victims of the Communist regime and therefore included. A group that was not included, however, was the deserters. Because at this point they had not yet been legally rehabilitated, they were still not seen as 'unrightfully persecuted', and in order to be included in the memorial, each one of them would have had to apply for individual rehabilitation. Only then would they have been allowed to consider themselves covered by the cross. And, even then, side by side with their own torturers.

Ludwig saw nothing but further humiliation and scorn in all this. For him, what was going on was unbearable. If he was ever rehabilitated himself, his suffering would be remembered by a memorial also dedicated to his own tormentors, the war criminals who had tortured him and killed so many of his comrades. Clearly not only was it a disgrace that Nazis were included in the memorial but by stating that it was only for those 'unrightfully persecuted', the Foundation had deliberately excluded all deserters, because, unlike the included Nazis, they had not yet been rehabilitated and were still legally seen as ex-convicts. With those words the Foundation acknowledged that sentences passed by Nazi war courts were to be seen as legally correct. According to them, the war courts had had a right to exist.

So who are remembered by this cross as innocent victims of brutal dictatorships along with Jews, Roma and others? The Torgau executioner Franz Klose is one example; his colleague from Torgau-Brückenkopf, Commandant Friedrich Heinicke, another; and Camp Commandant Heinrich Remlinger a third. All three had been sentenced by the Waldheim Trials. But as they had been rehabilitated by the united Germany's parliament, these Nazis were now officially considered as victims of persecution on equal terms with people we more usually see mentioned as such.

Apart from this cross erected in memory of the many, for a long time a single person, the so-called Angel from Fort Zinna, was honoured by a memorial tablet – in this case unveiled at the town's Evangelical cemetery in 1996. The Foundation of Saxony Memorials also helped with the financing of this project, but this time they might have gone a step too far and even realised that themselves, as they were faced with heavy criticism. A forceful human rights campaign succeeded in having this shameless memorial removed.

But who was this 'angel' who, sentenced by a Soviet military court, had been detained in Torgau between 1950 and 1955 and who had been given this celestial title by fellow prisoners? In 1938, Nazi party member Professor Friedrich Timm had been asked to apply for a post as legal physician at the University of Jena, and it was his activities there which many years later began to haunt him. In fact, it looks like the doctor's white coat of the angel is quite heavily stained in brown. Two years before this memorial tablet had been put up, it had already come to public knowledge that this German academic had during the war been involved in a PhD dissertation on origin and race in connection with crime. Dr Timm, a Nazi party member since 1933, had given the task to Erich Wagner and had afterwards found this man's work 'very good'. What was special about Wagner's work was that the subject had been researched by focusing on tattoos which this concentration camp doctor had collected from 800 prisoners from different groups at Buchenwald. Apart from the support from Professor Timm, Wagner's research had had the dubious honour of awakening the interest of the infamous Ilse Koch – wife of a concentration camp commandant – in tattooed prisoners. This interest led to the production of souvenirs from human skin. It was skin from these prisoners that was later used in the production of attractive lampshades.

But the cross and Timm's memorial tablet were not the only dubious memorials in Saxony. A year-long painful conflict of interests between the political right and different groups of victims then began, and in time this conflict became increasingly bitter and entrenched. One of the issues was a permanent exhibition called 'Traces of Injustice' (*'Spuren des Unrechts'*) that was opened at Hartenfels castle at the centre of the town, also on the initiative of the Foundation. In this exhibition, visitors are told about past oppression, and the same conflict between different groups is apparent. Again, victims of Nazi ideology are pushed aside and those who suffered under the Communists are to the fore. Despite the massive difference in cruelty between the Nazi years and the Communist era, the two dictatorships are portrayed as two equal injustices – and, in reality, not even equal. Compared with how the years under the East German dictatorship are portrayed, there is a sense of trivialisation of the Third Reich.

Far from remembering only the true victims, here we also find the war judges and Gestapo people. Their Nazi past is comfortably 'forgotten' and, alongside the others, they are portrayed as victims of Communist injustice. The only thing that counts today is that they were sentenced by the Waldheim Trials and then lumped together and rehabilitated by the reunited Germany's so-called SED Injustice Law.

For the victims of the Nazis, this situation was unacceptable. They did not want to be mentioned alongside those people, and at the opening of the exhibition they protested vociferously but to no avail. Despite the fact that organisations like the Gestapo and SD are seen as the basic tools of Nazi evil, and despite the war judges' bloodstained past in the service of Hitler, in this exhibition, according to the Foundation's statements, no war criminals are portrayed as victims, and with those words the case was closed.

It is not only the permanent exhibition and the problematic cross that for years have disturbed and haunted Ludwig and his friends. Persistent talks about a permanent memorial in front of Fort Zinna have been even more upsetting. It is not that Ludwig does not want a memorial. He would very much like one, but, as in previous examples, he does not want to share it with his tormentors. His long-term dream was and is a respectful memorial for all his murdered comrades; a place to go and remember. Yet what the Foundation persistently proposed was a memorial for them all, including the rehabilitated Nazis. Such a memorial at Fort Zinna would give a blanket dedication to all victim groups without further consideration, and there it would all end.

For years these plans were discussed by an advisory board established by the Foundation. This included a number of victim groups, among them the Central Council of Jews in Germany, represented by Ignatz Bubis, and the Federal Association of Victims of Military Justice, represented by Ludwig. In these meetings Ludwig was exposed to animosity on numerous occasions from those representing the East German victims.

> It was remarkable, but the chairperson, who was always one of them, spoke almost intimately about 'Adolf'. He spoke [with compassion] about 'Adolf's military justice' that had to handle such people who had been accused of cowardice when facing the enemy.

On one occasion, Ludwig was even accused of representing the interests of the deserters so strongly because he suffered from the fact he had not been shot himself. Not many raised their voices in his defence when he was attacked in that way. Bubis did.

It was the same problem as with the castle exhibition and the cross. Again, if the plans were allowed to go ahead, the deserters and other victims of the Nazis would see themselves alongside war criminals. The protests were intense and impassioned, and Ludwig fought against any plan to include his group in such a monument. Together with other victim groups, he found it humiliating that the Foundation of Saxony Memorials was continuing to put him together with the very same people who had tortured him and killed so many of this comrades.

Ludwig was not alone in his struggle. Other victim groups felt the same, and there was also support from the other side. A working group for memorial sites at earlier concentration camps also had serious objections to the plans. According to them, it sounded as if it was no longer important to consider the fact that Nazism was an entirely homemade evil, contrary to the East German dictatorship that basically had been resting on the bayonets of the Red Army. They also saw the risk of a future in which history would be distorted, and feared the door to such a development was about to be opened.

Even on the international front voices were raised. ICMEMO is an international committee, connected to UNESCO, of museums dedicated to the memory of public crimes such as Nazism, totalitarian forms of Communism, apartheid, military dictatorships and others, one aim of which is to foster the responsible recording of history. In the development in Torgau they saw an attempt to put the memory of the people under central control; paradoxically, they saw a parallel with the politics of the former East German dictatorship itself.

Despite this, the project went ahead. On 9 May 2010, the memorial was officially unveiled with the wooden cross incorporated into the new design. As planned all along, it commemorates the real victims of the two dictatorships – and with them a large number of rehabilitated war criminals. But at least, thanks to Ludwig's lengthy protests, the Nazi war judges are now separated from their victims by a hornbeam hedge. Various changes have also been asked for at the castle exhibition. They have been promised, but nothing has yet happened.

'All commemoration in Torgau is controlled by representatives of the victims of the DDR dictatorship. Ever since its inception, and as a kind of birthright, these people have chaired the advisory board of the Foundation of Saxony Memorials. This is why, in spite of long-standing criticism, the visiting public is still not being told that among the rehabilitated DDR victims there were also Nazis and war judges. While the Foundation seems to have no problem finding money to commemorate the victims of Stasi, it appears to be much more difficult to find the – in no way unreasonable – expenses needed to clarify properly the circumstances around THE war justice. It is a disgrace that a dignified commemoration of the victims of Nazi military justice is still not possible in Torgau of all places – the one-time seat of the Reich War Court'

Ludwig Baumann, 3 June 2013

Chapter 27

Two Equal Evils?

Halbe

Ludwig Baumann is an optimistic man who has shown that almost anything is possible. As we have learned, for years he has struggled against overwhelming adversity and misfortune, but has never given up. He wants peace and reconciliation, and fortunately he is not alone. The Jewish Central Council sided with him in Torgau, and there are others joining forces elsewhere. For him they are all welcome. After all, there are many places where war resistance needs to be emphasised – in fact, everywhere. But, as Ludwig says, at one site in particular we must never forget what happened, and it is precisely here that future generations should be reminded that the catastrophe of the Second World War must never be allowed to be repeated.

In late spring 1945, the Red Army closed in on Berlin. It was the final stage of the war. The Ninth Army of the *Wehrmacht*, one of the last forces left to defend Hitler's bunker, was in serious trouble, entrapped by the Soviets in the forests south-east of Berlin. It was obvious that the war would soon be over, that further fighting was pointless, and that surrender was the only reasonable option. However, the commanders of these troops were obviously terrified of a future in Siberia. Therefore, completely disregarding how many lives it might cost, they decided to attempt to break through the Red Army lines and escape west in order to surrender to the Western Allies. Not only would this cowardice cost another 30,000 German soldiers' lives but the Soviets would suffer the same number of casualties, and 10,000 civilians would also die.

These events have over the years turned Halbe/Brandenburg into a very special and important place, a symbolic site for all proponents of a world of peace and reconciliation, and, it goes without saying, so it is for Ludwig as well. For him, Halbe is of the utmost importance, also because of its Waldfriedhof burial ground, which is partly a military cemetery, where sixty deserters have been laid to rest among innumerable other war graves.

But, unfortunately, the forest cemetery in Halbe has been an important site not only for the peace movement: for many years in November, on People's Mourning Day, thousands of old and new Nazis used to gather here from all over the country. They turned the war graves into a major pilgrimage site. These events, which came about in the wake of the dissolved DDR, were a huge cause for concern for the future, so Ludwig was there among the protesting peace activists and anti-Fascists. Young and old stood together, and among them was also another elderly man, Franz von Hammerstein.

'Young men, who already in 1942 had the courage to stop fighting, rest in these graves. As far as I can remember from all the ceremonies held here, they have never ever been mentioned by any of the speakers.'

Ernst Teichmann, priest at Waldfriedhof cemetery, Halbe, from 1950 to 1983

Von Hammerstein was well known in peace circles in Germany and had had a special relationship to the war. As colonel general, his father had served in the armed forces of the Weimar Republic, but, as an honest and unwavering opponent of the Nazis, he had, contrary to so many of his colleagues, among them von Stauffenberg, followed his conscience and resigned in 1933, the year that Hitler came to power. Von Hammerstein's father had realised that the defence forces would be unable to resist Nazi influence; he could no longer be part of them and joined the resistance movement. The young Franz had two brothers, and they had also joined in the organised opposition to Hitler, later taking part in the planning of the 20 July assassination attempt. Following the failed attempt, they managed to escape and survived.

Franz, the third son, was equally devoted to peace. After the war, he was for many years a trustee of *Aktion Sühnezeichen/Friedensdienste*, a well-known German organisation committed to peace, social inclusion, anti-discrimination and anti-racism. It was in this context that his path would one day cross Ludwig's. From then on, the two men stood together and, among other things, they worked for a dignified memorial for Hitler's war resisters in Halbe/Brandenburg. Here, at the site of the last big battle of the war, would be a symbol for reconciliation; here, they thought, the struggle for a peaceful future would be strengthened.

In recent years, the political situation at the cemetery has been changed for the better; the neo-Nazi activities have been stopped and plans for both a special site of remembrance and a centre for peace education are being discussed. There is therefore a hope that Ludwig's and the now late Franz von Hammerstein's plan will one day be realised. Ludwig is convinced that if it is, it will send a strong message to future generations that refusing to go to war must be a human right.

A new perception of traitors

But what is the reason why, well into the twenty-first century, every attempt to debate the role of the *Wehrmacht* has been opposed as forcefully as we have seen in the previous chapters? After all, it is difficult to support the claim that these men, the so-called war traitors, betrayed their country.

Since 2007, a comprehensive work by Wolfram Wette and Detlef Vogel has been available about the issue of German war treason during the Second World War, and this work was extremely useful for the campaigners and political proponents of the final rehabilitation law. Wette and Vogel analysed a large number of sentences passed for war treason, and their conclusion was clear: the victims of the military courts had been mainly ordinary soldiers, and the 'crimes' committed were far from what would normally be associated with treason. Why had the rehabilitation of those people been such a sensitive issue? What had they actually done to earn themselves the epithet 'traitor', and what was it that made so many influential people continue to try to block their rehabilitation?

According to Wette and Vogel, some of the sentenced men had written and distributed leaflets in which they spoke out in favour of ending the war. In other cases, people had had contact with prisoners of war in an inappropriate way, i.e. they had helped them in one way or another. An example of a perpetrator who had done just that was the lorry driver Adolf Pogede. He had tried to save some Jews from the Holocaust. For that crime he was seen, until 2009, as a traitor to his nation. The archives contain many more examples of offences that qualified as treason.

In order to understand what lay behind the general mood and view on these matters all these years after the war, we need to go back in time. Among the officers of the armed forces there had been strong support not only for extreme nationalism and chauvinism but also for anti-Semitism and fanatical anti-Communism. The common view was that the 'elite' of the armed forces profoundly disliked not only the Weimar democracy but also pacifism and the pursuit of social justice and equality. What the 'traitors' had done was to act in sharp contravention of such values. Even after the war was over, these human values would not stand much chance of being heard. To a large degree, the same people who had ruled society would continue to pull the strings, and it was their voices that would be heard and listened to.

In Nuremberg, a defence strategy unfolded, and Albert Speer in particular developed into a master of its use. The basic 'truth' from now on was that Hitler, Himmler and Goebbels had been the culprits; the *Einsatzgruppen* and SS had been the criminal organisations. As they were the guilty ones, everyone else, as a consequence, must be innocent. The worst one could say about those innocent individuals was that they had been misled, that they had dutifully continued doing their job, though, in hindsight, they should not have done. It was a smart new tactic, and it was successful not least because so many would benefit from it and see themselves exculpated. But in order to succeed with this whitewash, other groups had to be kept silent, among them the deserters and war traitors. It was not in the interests of this new view on guilt for these other people to show that there had been another way.

It was clear at the start of the second Nuremberg process that the myth of the innocent armed forces and Foreign Office had been created and transformed into an established 'fact'. From now on, nothing would be allowed to challenge that view. This was how people wanted these institutions to be regarded, and they were seen in this way for decades after the war. So the small guys, those expected to obey, were to be labelled as the Nazi war criminals, not the big guys, those giving the orders in foreign occupied countries. Again, it was a class struggle, where the buck would be passed to the ordinary man. The desired view was of the proletarian Nazi thug on one side and the educated and decent gentleman on the other – in this equation, victims and perpetrators often swapped places.

This was the picture that Konrad Adenauer and his friends were more than happy with. This view of the world allowed the first Chancellor of West Germany to welcome a large number of Nazis, among them Hans Globke and Theodor Oberländer, back into public office. This was not only a development supported by the right-wing government, it was more or less the policy of the post-war political establishment. Very few dissident voices were heard. And it had support among the general population as well; after all, most people wanted to draw a line under it all. Adenauer felt that the majority of Germans had more sympathy for the locked-up war criminals than for the victims of the Nazis, and, as this was most likely true. Few protested when the conservative government acted on behalf of people like the two grand admirals Dönitz and Raeder (both serving time at Spandau) and Konstantin von Neurath, the former Nazi foreign minister.

As we have seen, the general view was that there had been only a handful of guilty men; all the others were victims themselves. First they had all been misled and abused by Hitler, and then they had been made to suffer from the war, and, as if that was not enough, at the end they had had to go through the ordeal of the 'unjust' denazification process. 'To be honest, are there no worse problems to worry about?' it was generally said, and they meant the Reds, as the Browns had disappeared overnight (or had at least changed colour). The nation now had to focus on the Communist threat, it was proclaimed in the western part of the former Third Reich, and, do not forget, that had been Hitler's agenda as well. For this job, there was a need for the old 'elite'. West Germany needed its anti-Communist experts, and what did it matter that many of these people were old friends of Goebbels and Himmler? It was now time to move on; it was time to stop blaming Hitler's patriots.

As Chancellor Adenauer said in a 1948 speech:

> The treatment in the British zone [of occupation] of the previously active officers [in the *Wehrmacht*] is unfair; it is wrong and, when looking at the future political development, grossly deplorable. It is unacceptable that *Wehrmacht* officers and officials who in an honest and decent way did their duty, just as their French, British and American counterparts did, are being defamed for that.

When we look at things from that perspective, it is easier to see the background that led to the reinstallation of the old guard. In the shadow of the Communist threat, it was better to clean up, forget and forgive. What did it matter that the German army had committed war crimes in Russia and elsewhere in the east? What did it matter that the Red Army had contributed hugely to the fall of the Nazis?

This view on the past and present in the early post-war years helped to establish the concept of Communism and Nazism as two equal evils – one of only historical interest, the other still remaining (for Germans in the DDR). The foundation had been laid not only for the old Nazis' return to powerful positions in society but also for the painful struggle for decent memorials in the post-Communist society in the east.

Konrad Adenauer.

Chapter 28

Political Turncoats

On 17 May 2002, after long campaigning by the Federal Association of Victims of Military Justice, the Social Democratic/Green coalition government finally enacted a law that would annul the sentences against the deserters. However, as it turned out, even after this victory by a thin majority – very far from an enthusiastic unanimous decision – not all the victims of Hitler's military courts had been rehabilitated. The final text had been amended before the law had finally been allowed to pass, and one major group of victims as well as three smaller groups had been removed. In the text that was enacted as law, people who had been sentenced for having helped the enemy, the so-called *Kriegsveräter* (war traitors), were no longer included, and the same was the case for individuals who, while on military duty, had been sentenced for pillage, stealing from the dead, and mistreatment of a subordinate.

While having been nudged into rehabilitating the deserters, the governing parties were still not ready to approve a blanket rehabilitation of all remaining victims. When it came to those left out, the government, in line with the conservative opposition, remained adamant: each and every case would have to be individually looked at. As most of these soldiers were long dead, and all records were the products of the military courts and their investigators, it is easy to understand that a probe into individual cases remained the impossible task it had always been. Apart from that, as before, this would have been intrinsically wrong. Any post-war legal probe into individual sentences would have been equivalent to recognition of the Nazi court's fundamental right to have existed.

In what follows I will use the term 'war treason' as opposed to 'high treason'. According to German law at the time, and before, there were two kinds of treason: high treason and war treason (*Hochverrat* and *Kriegsverrat* respectively). War treason applied mainly to military personnel and could be translated more accurately as 'aiding the enemy'. However, what is important to remember is that people sentenced for high treason during the war had long since been rehabilitated by the state. Only war treason remained as a legitimately punishable treason offence. Only when it came to war treason (legislation that had been made more severe by Hitler's regime) German law, political parties and society would still regard Hitler's courts as legitimate courts passing legitimate sentences. The reason for this was the usual: 'The sentences cannot be annulled, as we cannot exclude the possibility that lives of German soldiers may have been put in danger because of their comrades-in-arms aiding the enemy.'

Before we concentrate on the main group, the war traitors, let us consider the remaining three categories of alleged offenders not worthy of blanket rehabilitation. Despite the war being nothing if not mass murder in which the German state and its institutions not only plundered and stole from millions of dead victims but also extremely cruelly mistreated its own conscripts, those ordinary soldiers who had been charged and sentenced for doing the same on a more personal level, whether true or not, would continue to be seen as rightfully punished and not worthy of having their sentences annulled. As we have seen, in 2002, Hitler's law was still legally binding, and a large majority of the parliament had shown no interest in changing that.

Let us now look at different acts of 'criminal behaviour' that would have been defined as war treason by Nazi military courts. Betrayal of German expansionist plans in occupied countries was of course an offence that would have qualified, but there was much more to it than that. It could have been attempting to inform the outside world about the murder of Jews; or trying to save the lives of persecuted people; or just giving a piece of extra food to a Russian prisoner of war. Maybe the perpetrator had done nothing more than innocently writing in his diary about a Jewish or Bolshevik friend. All that, and much more of the same, would have defined him as a war traitor and made him eligible for severe punishment. This is not an attempt to trivialise crime. Recent research by the historian Wolfram Wette has clarified that the so-called war traitors had generally acted ethically and in a politically correct way. In fact, not a single example of what we would call criminal action has been found among the large number of cases that have been investigated.

Though Ludwig Baumann, with the passing of the rehabilitation law of 2002, had been rehabilitated himself, he had not achieved his goal. He could not accept the fact that not all his former comrades had been rehabilitated, and therefore the struggle continued and would go on for another seven years. But it was an uphill struggle, and the chance that this man, who had fought so long for justice, would ever see this group of sentenced soldiers also rehabilitated was indeed not great.

> 'Without dignity a human being cannot live.'
>
> *Ludwig Baumann*

This is where *Die Linke* (The Left), a small left-wing party with roots in the undemocratic 'Democratic' republic, the DDR, would re-enter the picture and level the playing field. In 2005, Ludwig and his hardworking Federal Association secretary and fellow campaigner Günter Knebel had informed them – as well as other parties – about the situation, and, as a result, the newly elected Member of Parliament Jan Korte joined the efforts and became Ludwig's man in Berlin. At last there was a politician in the *Bundestag* who, with all his heart, would stand up for the military victims of the Third Reich. It had taken sixty years to get to that point, but here he was.

Two photographs of Johann Lukaschitz. *Courtesy of Gedenkstätte Roter Ochse, Halle*

In 2009, the von Stauffenberg film *Valkyrie* with Tom Cruise in the leading role was shown all over the world as well as in Germany. Unquestionably, this led to strong emotions being evoked – not least among those who were old enough and able enough to see behind the glorifying curtain of the film industry. As one of those, when Ludwig walked past the huge posters he was full of bitterness and despair, the same feelings that had followed him most of his life but which had now suddenly come to the fore – due to this worldwide celebration of a Nazi German officer turned (unsuccessful) assassinator and hero.

After all, how was it possible that Hollywood could honour as an undisputed hero an aristocrat like Colonel Claus Schenk Graf von Stauffenberg, who had served Hitler loyally for twelve years before trying to kill him, when an ordinary conscripted soldier – who, during the same conflict, might have expressed a few critical remarks about the regime or maybe had helped a Jew or prisoner of war – sixty-four years after the slaughter had ended, was still seen as a traitor?

'How can it be that von Stauffenberg was being glorified, when Johann was still seen as a traitor?' Ludwig asked himself. Johann Lukaschitz was twenty-four when Ludwig met him, and he did not live to be any older. He was from Vienna, and for some days he was in the next bed to Ludwig in the hospital ward at Fort Zinna, Torgau. As Ludwig remembers, he was a quiet, gentle and thoughtful person, but he was in serious trouble. Johann's wrists and ankles were bloody as a consequence of the heavy chains he was forced to wear, but it did not stop there: he had been sentenced to death because he had not reported an act of treason. When a group of soldiers had formed a secret group, Johann had not taken part, but he knew about it, and now, because he had not informed on his friends, he had been charged with war treason himself. Judge Werner Lueben had sealed Johann's fate on 3 February 1944, and eight days later he was decapitated.

This move would make the difference in the end, but it would also put further focus on the serious left–right divide on this controversial issue. Just as was the case with ex-Communist parties in other western European countries at the time, there was no undemocratic Communist ideology in *Die Linke*. For its opponents, however, this fact was easily disregarded. In spite of all the Brown skeletons they had in their own wardrobes, some political parties further to the right would continue to see the socialists as untouchables.

Die Linke then drafted a new bill. However, as expected, the process through parliament was to be long and difficult and full of obstacles and delaying tactics. The vote against the bill was at first overwhelming – and that situation would not change easily. As late as 2006, Minister of Justice Brigitte Zypries, a Social Democrat, wrote to Ludwig and made it clear that the reason for not including the war treason sentences in the 2002 law was that 'the possibility cannot be excluded that the act [of treason] had endangered the lives of fellow soldiers and this risk would have been considerable'. As before, the fact that the alleged acts of betrayal and aiding the enemy had taken place on the aggressor's side of a war that was clearly in breach of international law was, according to the same logic, no reason to annul these sentences without individual scrutiny of each and every case. Right up until 2009, this was the astonishing political view of the CDU/CSU, the FDP (the Liberals) and the SPD (the Social Democrats). With her comment, Mrs Zypries had supported Hitler's alleged right not to have his armed forces infiltrated with people who would try to prevent him from fulfilling his ambitions.

Jan Korte was not unfamiliar with issues concerning victims of the war and post-war rehabilitation. Immediately after being elected to parliament, he started to campaign for justice for those who had been subject to gross discrimination in that field. In the 1950s, the young West German state had passed the *Bundesentschädigungsgesetz* (BEG), a compensation law for resistance fighters and victims of the Nazi dictatorship. However, in line with the growing anti-Communist sentiment in society at the time, pay-outs to Communists were refused or made conditional; if they wanted compensation to be paid, they were requested to leave the (fully legal) West German Communist Party, the KPD. Referring to this injustice, Korte had asked the government in power fifty years later for a comment. The reply he got was that there was no reason to look into the matter. The government kept to the position that had ruled this subject ever since the early days of the Federal Republic. There was no change in position.

Not only Communists were excluded. Another man who unsuccessfully applied to be compensated under the post-war BEG, the Federal Restitution Law, was Georg Bock. According to that law, Bock did not qualify as a legitimate victim of Nazi persecution. He was not seen as a proper opponent of Hitler. Therefore, his application for BEG compensation was refused. Pte Bock had refused to put out anti-personnel mines and had been punished for that. The reason for the refusal to compensate him for his suffering was as follows:

First, his act had caused only minor problems for the army; second, it is possible that his actions could have put other soldiers in danger (no thought was spared for the enemy soldiers who would step on the mines); third, his actions could have put his own family in danger (no compensation, because the Nazis might have gone for his family); and fourth, Pte Bock's actions did not weaken the Nazi regime. Therefore, he was not a victim.

Now Korte's work would focus on a slightly different matter, but the reaction was the same. In the first debate on its proposed legislation about the war traitors, *Die Linke* met determined resistance. This was an issue that was extremely important for the far right of the political sphere, and no effort would be spared to defend the status quo. Hardliners were brought out to defend the position, and with dramatic speeches they vowed to fight against any attempt to rehabilitate the 'traitors'. Even the Liberals (FDP) took this position, as did the Social Democrats, as we have seen. It was an uphill struggle, and in parliament only the Green Party supported their left-wing colleagues. From all other sides they were met with rejection or, even worse, a wall of silence. The media also joined in that silence; apart from a left-wing newspaper, no journalists would report anything about the subject despite strenuous efforts from Korte's side to get them interested.

However, things were about to happen. The issue started to burden the big parties. Therefore, while officially opposing any change, the Ministry of Justice, behind the scenes, led by a Social Democrat in a broad coalition with the CDU/CSU, was looking into the question. Was there a need for change in position? How could they deal with this issue without losing face and votes? It was all very uncertain. There were some signs of movement, but real change still seemed distant. At the time it seemed like a game was being played in order to keep campaigners and *Die Linke* at bay.

On 5 May 2008, the parliamentary committee responsible for the proposed law had arranged a hearing. At this hearing, it was obvious that the Social Democrats were sitting on the fence, waiting to see which side would be more convenient to join. Though officially against the new legislation, they had invited both Ludwig and Professor Manfred Messerschmidt as experts. To counter them the Conservatives had asked the military historian Professor Rolf-Dieter Müller to join the panel.

Müller more than fulfilled the political right's expectations, as he criticised the Wette research that was now widely used by the proponents of the bill as the basis for a change in position. 'Even after this publication, there is nothing new about the issue of [Second World War] war treason,' the professor claimed, continuing: 'The examples Wette has put forward are most likely exceptions rather than the rule.' Furthermore it was the professor's opinion that leaking of military secrets (i.e. Nazi secrets also) is treason and must be punished. In order to clarify his point, he used the example of Edgar Feuchtinger. Though this had been an ordinary soldier's offence, Müller used the example of a general.

Feuchtinger had been commander of an armoured division, but the general had other interests as well. His girlfriend was a dancer and, to make things worse, she was South American. Of course, what Feuchtinger had done was far from patriotic – after all, it had happened in the midst of a world war – he had used his power to supply his foreign lover with valuable and scarce petrol from the army so that she could drive leisurely around Germany in between seeing him. But, even worse, in letters to this woman, Feuchtinger had disclosed military secrets, and he had to pay a price for that. He was reported, court-martialled – according to Müller for war treason – and sentenced to death.

However, after the committee hearing was over, Müller was asked for evidence. As he could not present any, another expert witness, Helmut Kramer, searched the archives in Freiburg and was able to establish that there were no such documents to be found. In the general's file there was no trace of such a sentence. Kramer again requested Müller to present evidence for his statement, and the CDU/CSU expert witness was left with no other option than to admit that he was unable to. He had taken his unverified information from a book (*Abgehört* by Sönke Neitzel, published in 2007) and from a statement made by a war court judge in 1963.

End of story: there had been no sentence for war treason; the professor had invented this version himself. The general had not been sentenced for treason but for *Wehrkraftzersetzung*, because, against the rules, he had spent time with his girlfriend in Paris. It was for that offence, not for war treason, that he had been sentenced. If Müller had given himself time, he could have read that himself in the same book, and, if that was not embarrassing enough for the expert, he should also have known that the general had already been automatically rehabilitated for that crime – through the 1998 law that had annulled all sentences for *Wehrkraftzersetzung*.

Three years after this self-humiliating appearance at the parliamentary law committee hearing, Müller was appointed as an expert adviser in the secret services' reprocessing of documents regarding the Klaus Barbie case. Barbie, Gestapo member and Nazi army captain, also known as the 'Butcher of Lyon', was in a high-profile case years after the conflict, finally charged with war crimes in France. However, before the arm of French justice finally reached him, Barbie is alleged to have been employed not only by US intelligence services but also (post-war) by their German counterparts. Now documents regarding that past were to be re-evaluated, and Müller was obviously the right man for the job. It is difficult to find any better argument against individual investigation of each war traitor's case than Müller's performance at the hearing and his subsequent appointment.

Yet this man had not been the only CDU/CSU expert witness at the hearing. Sönke Neitzel, history professor and author of the above-mentioned book referred to by Müller, was another. Neitzel also presented an individual example in order to build his case against a blanket rehabilitation. His point was – and we have heard this before – that an act of treason would have endangered the lives of German soldiers. In order to win the argument, this professor referred to two marine officers who had revealed to the enemy all they knew about a top-secret acoustic torpedo. Astonishingly enough, according to Neitzel, this torpedo, the T-5, was a defensive weapon. Because of the disclosures, which had been given during interrogations, the Allies had been able to take precautions against this highly effective 'defensive' weapon.

Again it was Helmut Kramer who would point out that something was wrong. As with the case of Rolf-Dieter Müller, Professor Neitzel could not, against all academic rules, present any kind of evidence for his claim that the two submariners had been sentenced for war treason. This man, who obviously saw it as a despicable act to inform the Allied forces fighting Nazi Germany about new highly effective torpedoes, now teaches students at the London School of Economics.

'Disloyalty to war is loyalty to peace.'

Ludwig Baumann

However, a change of position was taking place at least within the Social Democratic Party, one of the three governing parties. Their originally dismissive view on the matter was gradually changing; it was not as clear as it had been. After all, there was an ongoing fight for the political centre stage in the country, and party political opinions are steered by what people want to hear. In line with that, it was important to deal with this controversial issue, rather than let it impact negatively on the upcoming election.

As the bill then was up for its second reading in the *Bundestag*, the pressure had increased even further on all three coalition parties: the CDU/CSU Conservative union and the Social Democratic SPD. They all wanted this issue swept under the carpet. They had even reached the point where they would let it pass, if only to prevent it from haunting them, but, as before, it was clear that none of those coalition parties would vote for the proposed law. The reason? Because it had been introduced by Oskar Lafontaine's *Die Linke* party. The big parties would not allow *Die Linke* a political success; they would not support anything proposed by them. Therefore, behind the scenes, things were happening – a solution was sought.

Brigitte Zypries' Ministry of Justice had at this point already made its first unofficial attempt to get *Die Linke* to withdraw their bill, so that the coalition government could put it forward as their own. There is no question that this remarkable change of position in government policy was due not only to direct political lobbying but also to increasing media interest. Journalists had entered the stage, increased the pressure and made the government's previous position untenable. Thanks to the persistent work of Jan Korte and not least the people around him – Dominic Heilig, Ludwig Baumann and Günter Knebel – the media had woken up, even to some extent the international media.

For Korte, the spokesperson for the small left-wing party, any solution that would bring about rehabilitation was acceptable. Unusually in political life, not only in Germany but elsewhere, for him it was far more important to get the law passed than to take credit for it. For the sake of the cause, *Die Linke* therefore suggested that all parties represented in parliament should together put forward and endorse the new bill.

Such a suggestion, in spite of its exceptional graciousness, did not suit the right-wing CDU/CSU. To join forces with *Die Linke*, especially in an election year and on a subject as controversial as this, was out of the question. But they had to do something. The pressure had increased after the disastrous performance of their expert witness Müller, and it was clear that in the long term they would not succeed in their attempt to deny rehabilitation to the last victims of the military courts. The Christian Democrats (CDU) and their sister party in Bavaria (CSU) were looking for a way out of the mess, but they could not be seen to be walking hand in hand with *Die Linke*.

Then an initiative came from the Social Democrats, the SPD. The matter was 'a most important issue for the party', it was suddenly announced; 'a core issue'. After years of dismissal and, at most, lukewarm interest, they were now ready to take the lead in the struggle for rehabilitation. Korte and *Die Linke* had assiduously worked and campaigned for years, battling against the tide, but now, listening to the newly converted, it was as if Korte and his party hardly existed. Others were coming in to take the credit. For the young left-wing parliamentarian this unbelievable political betrayal must have been extremely difficult to swallow. But for Korte it was all about the cause of rehabilitation of the war 'traitors' and not about personal success.

As a bill introduced by *Die Linke* would not be supported, Korte made a new attempt to achieve a breakthrough. He asked the Social Democrats and the Greens to join *Die Linke* in a joint proposal. A new bill, very similar to the existing one, was drafted and signatures were collected. On 17 June 2009, all *Die Linke* and Green members of parliament as well as forty-nine SPD people and two members from the further right parties had signed. However, though it further increased the pressure, this attempt also failed.

As the parliamentary term neared its end, behind the scenes there was intensive work going on. Interest in settling the issue was at its height. All of a sudden one more legislative proposal was put forward. The CDU/CSU had finally concluded that they were fighting a losing battle and were about to lose face. They had to prevent a *Die Linke* success. With the constructed argument that 'rehabilitation would be legally correct, as it was now impossible to verify the [individual] motivation behind these people's actions', the Conservatives changed their position and invited the Social Democrats, the Liberals and the Greens to join them in a third bill – again, one almost identical to the first. All these parties accepted the offer and so a new proposal was put forward by almost the entire *Bundestag*. Only *Die Linke* and Korte, precisely those who had worked so long and so hard to push this question, were not allowed to join in promoting the bill.

On 8 September 2009, on the very last day of parliament, all *Bundestag* parties (including *Die Linke* of course) voted in favour of this law. Korte had not been allowed to put his name to the text that finally annulled the last Nazi war court sentences, but it was his work; it was his achievement. It was he who had finally pushed parliament to stop recognising the Nazi war courts as legitimate courts of justice and distance itself from Hitler.

As with so many others in this story who did what was right, Korte never got the credit for it. That is a scandal. But the even bigger scandal is the fact that a debate like the one in September 2009 had been necessary at all. Hitler's 'justice' should have been declared null and void by late 1945.

A controversial exhibition

One Friday afternoon in Munich City Hall, hundreds of people carefully watch the *Wehrmachtsausstellung*, the controversial 1995-2004 exhibition of war crimes committed by the German armed forces during the Second World War. A dignified man with grey hair is speaking to a school class from Pasing. He looks sombre, calm, but matter-of-fact. The children listen attentively.

Ludwig Baumann regrets nothing he did then, he says, even though he had to sit shackled in his death cell for ten months, daily expecting his execution. He regrets nothing, even if the nightmare still haunts him. It is so many years ago, but he still wakes up drenched in sweat. Someone has banged on the cell door again. In his dream he is always sure: this time they are coming for him; this time they will take him out to be shot. In sleep, Ludwig is back at Fort Zinna in Torgau – at the mercy of the judges and guards.

Ludwig Baumann by the memorial 'The Unknown Deserter' in Bremen-Vegesack. 'We were threatened and smeared as cowards and traitors. But had there been more of us, the war would have been over much sooner. Millions of people would not have had to die.'

This is the deserter's trauma, his lifelong, nightly hell. For Ludwig it has been a long struggle against horrible memories; a struggle for recognition and legal rehabilitation, but most of all, it has been and still is a persistent struggle for a peaceful future. 'I have learned from my history that we must never let ourselves be seduced into attacking others.' Again and again he tells his story. Refusal to go to war must be acknowledged as a human right.

· · · · ·

'"No more war" is the legacy of our victims.'

Ludwig Baumann

Chapter 29

In Memory

Complete military loyalty to Adolf Hitler was the very foundation of the Nazi war of aggression. Without this loyalty the Second World War and the Holocaust would never have been possible. However, thousands of people discovered that they were participating in genocide and deserted. There were also those who never got that far: they refused outright to swear the oath to an evil despot. In memory of all these opponents of the Nazi military forces, the Peace Library and Anti-War Museum of the Evangelical Church in Berlin-Brandenburg has provided these portraits and short stories for this book. Together with the photograph of the execution they are part of the small museum's mobile exhibition *Kriegsdienstverweigerung im dritten Reich* (War Resistance in the Third Reich) in memory of all deserters and conscientious objectors under the Nazi dictatorship.

Hermann Stöhr was born on 4 January 1898 in Stettin and served as a soldier throughout the First World War. From 1923, he was active in the International Alliance of Reconciliation. In 1936, he founded a small publishing house and, in 1939, he refused to follow the call-up to the Nazi German armed forces. In August of that year, Stöhr was arrested and sentenced to one year in prison. Still refusing to swear the oath of loyalty to Hitler after having served his sentence, he was sentenced to death and executed by beheading at Berlin-Plötzensee Prison on 16 March 1940.

Max Josef Metzger, whose father was a schoolteacher, was born on 3 February 1887 at Schopfheim in the Black Forest. He was ordained a Catholic priest in 1911 and served as an army chaplain during the First World War. From 1917, he was an active and leading figure in national and international peace groups and contributed in 1919 to the foundation of the missionary association 'The White Cross' in Graz. From 1933 to 1943, Metzger was arrested repeatedly by the Gestapo and on 14 October 1943 he was sentenced to death for furthering the cause of the enemy because of having issued a peace memorandum. Metzger was executed by beheading at Brandenburg-Görden on 17 April 1944.

'Today it's a month ago since I stood in front of the People's Court. There were seven of us. Very soon after the trial had started, I was left with the clear conviction that here the truth was not to be looked for; it was all a show trial. I was in no doubt that there was no reason for hope; the decision had already been taken before I was to

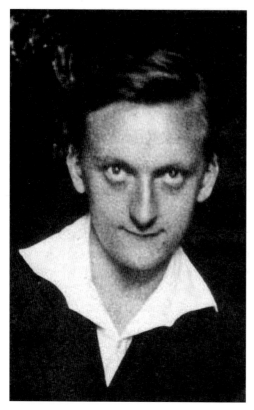

Hermann Stöhr.

Max Josef Metzger.

be given a chance to defend myself. Then, at the moment I heard the death sentence handed out, a feeling of proud contempt filled me. I knew that it was no shame but an honour to be declared dishonourable and be sentenced to death by such a court. In no way was I affected by it.'

Max Josef Metzger, 14 November 1943

Martin Gauger, the son of a vicar in Wuppertal, was born on 4 August 1905. After his studies he worked as an assessor for the prosecution at the local court – until he refused to swear the oath to Hitler and was sacked. In April 1940, Gauger also refused to follow the draft to the armed forces and tried to escape to Holland. The attempt was unsuccessful: he was arrested by the SS and severely injured in the process. After having been held at the Buchenwald concentration camp, Gauger was finally transferred to Pirna-Sonnenstein where he was executed by gas in 1941.

'For a while I thought I could endure this war, as I didn't have to fight with weapons. But that was a . ong and completely narrow-minded way of looking at it. Today I see it differently: one must not in any way do war service, at least not in this war,

Martin Gauger.

because it's not a defensive war. To start with I saw it as a relief when I was assigned to the commissariat: I wouldn't have to serve with arms. But, after having thought about it, what difference does it really make in the end if one fights oneself or if one just supplies those who do? No, it's all the same; no, I cannot support this war. I cannot accept that my work will help drown other countries with blood and tears.'

Martin Gauger, April 1940

Franz Jägerstätter was born on 20 May 1907 in St Radegund in Upper Austria where he grew up on a farm. Jägerstätter married in 1936 and continued to run the farm. In spring 1938, after the German occupation of Austria, he was the only person in the village to vote 'no' in the plebiscite that followed. In 1940, he was drafted to the Nazi German armed forces and returned home in April 1941. On 23 February the following year he was redrafted, but this time he did not follow the order. He was arrested on 2 March and at that point he declared that his Catholic beliefs prevented him from doing war service. On 6 July he was sentenced to death by beheading by the Reich War Court in Berlin and was executed at Brandenburg-Görden on 9 August 1943.

Franz Jägerstätter.

'Will just write a few words which come from the bottom of my heart. I am writing with my hands in shackles, but it's still easier than if the restraint had also been applied to my mind. Is it not a mockery when we ask God for peace although we don't want any? If we really did, we should just put down our weapons. How can it possibly be a crime or a sin when someone as a Catholic simply refuses military duty, even if that refusal for him would mean an even more certain death? Wouldn't it under such circumstances be much more in line with the Christian faith to sacrifice oneself in the first place rather than – in order to try and stay alive a bit longer – to participate in the murders of others, people who also have a right to live in this world?'

Franz Jägerstätter (from his death cell, 1943)

Josef Ruf was born in Saulgau on 15 December 1905, the son of an official in the state railway. After having received his certificate of completed apprenticeship as a tailor in 1925, he lived until 1933 in various Franciscan monasteries before joining the Christian community of *Christkönigsgesellschaft*. In spring 1940, at the age of thirty-five, he was drafted to Pinkafeld in Styria, Austria, and refused to swear the oath to Adolf Hitler because of his Christian beliefs. As a consequence, in September the same year he was sentenced to death for *Wehrkraftzersetzung* by the Reich War Court in Berlin and was executed by beheading on 10 October 1940 at Brandenburg-Görden.

Josef Ruf.

Gustav Stange.

Gustav Stange was trained as a cobbler and lived in Stuttgart until 1942, when he was drafted for war duty. He refused because his membership of the Jehovah's Witnesses forbade him to swear the oath to Hitler. His case was handled by the war tribunal in Stuttgart, and on 20 February 1942, Stange was sentenced to death and executed the same day. He is buried without a headstone outside the *Steinhaldenfriedhof* cemetery in Stuttgart.

'On conscientious grounds Gustav Stange categorically refused to serve as a soldier; he would under no circumstances swear an oath of loyalty to Adolf Hitler. He knew where 'On conscientious grounds Gustav Stange categorically refused to serve as a soldier; he would under no circumstances swear an oath of loyalty to Adolf Hitler. He knew where he stood on this matter and couldn't be swayed. To the captain's question during the trial "What would happen if all people were to do what you have done?" he answered: "Then the war would immediately end."'

Rudolf Daur, 1950

Deserteurslied

(Music and words by Peter Schilling; English interpretation by Josephine Doorley-Petersson)

Ein Lied hab ich euch mitgebracht,
Das niemand gern will hören,
Ich sing es manchmal in der Nacht, (repeat)
Dies Lied von Deserteuren.

Es war einmal vor langer Zeit,
Ein Mensch, der sollt marschieren,
Doch dazu war er nicht bereit, (repeat)
Er wollte nicht parieren.

Dort ist der Feind, so sagten sie,
Und den musst du erschlagen.
Doch er sagt nein, das tu ich nie, (repeat)
Drum ging's ihm an den Kragen.

Man brachte ihn vors Kriegsgericht,
Dort kann man keine Gnade …
Wem es an Pflichtgefühl gebricht, (repeat)
Um den ist's auch nicht schade!

Da half kein Bitten und kein Flehn,
Man kannte kein Erbarmen.
Er starb als Held, ich hab's gesehn, (repeat)
Am Strick der Feldgendarmen.

Ein anderer kam vors Standgericht,
Denn er war kriegsverdrossen.
Das kümmerte die Richter nicht, (repeat)
Er wurde bald erschossen.

Ich singe, was noch stets geschieht,
Ich sing von Heldentaten,
Denn es erzählt mein kleines Lied (repeat)
Von Richtern und Soldaten.

Ich sing von der Aufmüpfigkeit,
Ich sing von Deserteuren,
Vom Henkersstrick und großem Leid, (repeat)
Doch wer will das schon hören.

Ich such mir selber Freund und Feind,
Und lass mir's nicht befehlen,
Denn was uns trennt und uns vereint, (repeat)
Das will ich selber wählen.

The Deserter's Song

Please listen to my song today,
Please listen to my truth,
It haunts me often in the night, (repeat)
The horrors of my war-torn youth.

There was a time some years ago,
A man was told to march,
But no, he won't, he told them so, (repeat)
Oh, no; oh, no, he would not go.

The war court was then next for Fritz,
And nothing there was just,
For if you fail your Fatherland, (repeat)
You know we will do what we must.

'Oh, what a coward,' the lawyer said,
'You didn't play your role.
'This is no country for your kind, (repeat)
'You haven't got our type of soul.'

The young man died before my eyes,
I can't forget his cries.
That's what they did to German youth (repeat)
Who didn't share the Führer's truth.

I sing about an awful war,
When terror merged with law,
I sing about the hangman's rope, (repeat)
And gruesome horrors that I saw.

So listen to me, one and all,
Defy the tyrant's call,
Choose your pal and choose your foe, (repeat)
And never let your freedom go.

Afterword

Thanks to hundreds of years of propaganda, a deserter in most countries is seen as a traitor, a coward who betrays his country and its people. All over the world this view is common and accepted. No consideration is given to the nature of the war from which the person had absconded. Was the own side's involvement of a purely defensive nature, or did it have a criminal, aggressive character? Did the young man let down his endangered fellow citizens of a peaceful democracy, or did he decline to assist the ruling 'elite' in their quest for increased power and control over other people? Rarely are those fundamental questions asked. It seems like the subject is taboo; beyond any serious discussion.

Not even a defector from the enemy's side can be sure of a welcome. They are all traitors, or so it seems. Unfortunately, as a consequence of this peculiar way of looking at loyalty, all around the world there are innumerable examples of young men who have lost not only their lives but also their honour as a consequence of going their own way – refusing to fight a war that was not theirs – and others are constantly being added to the very long list. Each and every one of these young men has his own biography, but most of them can be summed up with just a few words: a stolen life – all caused by circumstances over which the individual had had no say.

While writing this book, I constantly had a few lines from the works of the late Danish poet Halfdan Rasmussen in the back of my head. He wrote it for Amnesty International, and it is about torture. I will not claim that this book is strictly about torture, though it could be argued that it contains a fair bit of it. However, what I would claim is that Hitler's deserters, both during and after the war, were exposed to a treatment that was cruel, inhuman and degrading. All that, and torture, are often mentioned in the same sentence – as in the Universal Declaration of Human Rights, proclaimed and adopted on 10 December 1948 by the General Assembly of the United Nations. There it is written in Article 5 that 'no one shall be subjected to torture or to cruel, inhuman or degrading treatment or punishment'.

Rasmussen shared that view, but he also felt that there could be something even worse out there. I know it might be easy for somebody like me to say so (after all, I have never been tortured myself), but I do understand what this most beloved poet tried to say. Therefore, I would like to share his words with you in my own free and utmost humble English version:

It's not the torturer who scares me;
It's not the hate, suffering or pain.
Neither is it the rifle they might point at me,
Nor the ghastly shadows down the lane.
No, it's none of that which hurts me,
What it is is the blind indifference,
Yes, all those fellow human beings who do not give a damn.

Lars G. Petersson, June 2013

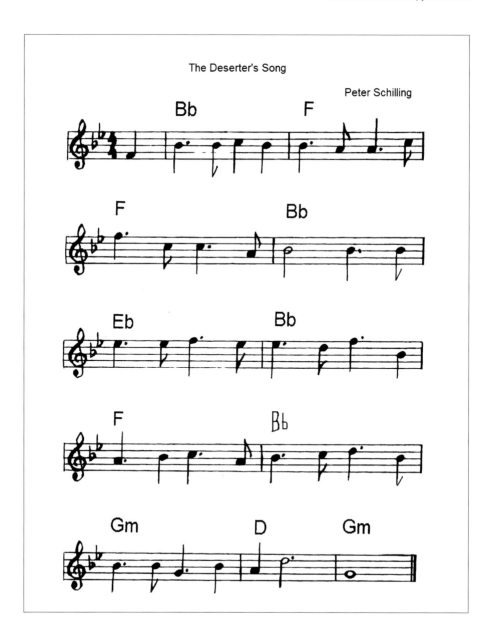

The Deserter's Song

Peter Schilling

Bibliography

Baumann, Ulrich, and Magnus Koch, Stiftung Denkmal für die ermordeten Juden Europas (ed.), *'Was damals Recht war ...' Soldaten und Zivilisten vor Gerichten der Wehrmacht*; Berlin-Brandenburg, 2008; (in German)

Berglund, Tobias, and Niclas Sennerteg, *Svenska koncentrationsläger i tredje rikets skugga*; Natur & Kultur, Stockholm, 2008; (in Swedish)

Heide, Eivind, *Deserteringer fra den tyske okkupasjonshæren i Norge 1940-1945*; Sollia, Oslo, 1995; (in Norwegian, Bokmål)

Kober, Helmut, *Jugend im dritten Reich, Erinnerung an Russland 1942/43*; Önel-Verlag, Cologne, 1993; (in German)

Korte, Jan, and Dominic Heilig (eds), *Kriegsverrat – Vergangenheitspolitik in Deutschland*; Karl Dietz, Berlin, 2011; (in German)

Kretschmann, Kurt, *Und da leben sie noch? Erinnerungen eines Deserteurs*; Friedensbibliothek/Antikriegsmuseum der Evangelischen Kirche in Berlin-Brandenburg, 1999; (in German)

Messerschmidt, Manfred, and Fritz Wüllner, *Die Wehrmachtjustiz im Dienste des Nationalsozialismus – Zerstörung einer Legende*; Nomos, Baden-Baden, 1987; (in German)

Messerschmidt, Manfred, *Die Wehrmachtjustiz 1933-1945*; Ferdinand Schöningh, Paderborn, 2005; (in German)

Müller, Ingo, *Furchtbare Juristen: Die unbewältigte Vergangenheit unserer Justiz*; Kindler-Verlag, Munich, 1987; (in German)

Röhm, Eberhard, *Sterben für den Frieden, Spurensicherung Hermann Stöhr*; Calwer, Stuttgart, 1985; (in German)

Schweling, Otto Peter, and Erich Schwinge, *Die deutsche Militärjustiz in der Zeit des Nationalsozialismus*; N. G. Elwert, Marburg, 1978; (in German)

Wette, Wolfram (ed.) *Das Letzte Tabu NS-Militärjustiz und Kriegsverrat*; Aufbau, Berlin, 2007; (in German)